Fathers in Families

T0353045

The role of the father in a family and for his children has varied greatly throughout history. However, scientific research into fatherhood began relatively late at the end of the 1960s and early 1970s, with a strong focus on the impact of the father on child development. This book focuses on the role of the father in the contemporary two-parent heterosexual family. Of eight longitudinal studies from several Western countries, six focus on the socialization outcomes of the children, and two concentrate on parental satisfaction. Although the father is in focus, family dynamics cannot be conclusively described without a look at the mother and parental interaction. Therefore, all of the studies examine mothers and their role in the family system. Thus, the book gives a contemporary insight into the father and his role in changing family dynamics.

This book was originally published as a special issue of the *European Journal of Developmental Psychology*.

Dorothea E. Dette-Hagenmeyer is a Research Associate in the Department of Psychology at the Ludwigsburg University of Education, Germany. She earned her Ph.D. from the Friedrich-Alexander-University Erlangen-Nuremberg, Germany. She conducted research into family (parenting, co-parenting, coping, close relationships), gender roles, work-life-balance, and evidence-based parenting programs and has a teaching record in research methods, developmental, social and positive psychology.

Andrea B. Erzinger achieved a Master's Degree in Education, Private Law and Political Science at the University of Zurich, Switzerland, and is currently a research assistant at the University of Teacher Education (PHSG), St. Gallen, Switzerland. Her research interests are social and emotional development over the life course, familial intergenerational relationships, school-family-interaction and development of competencies.

Barbara Reichle is Professor of Developmental and Educational Psychology at Ludwigsburg University of Education, Germany. She completed a Doctoral degree in Psychology from Trier University, Germany. Her research focuses on the socio-emotional development of children within families and schools, parenting, intimate relationships, the transition to parenthood, and justice in the family. She is co-author of two evidence-based evaluated prevention programs (attachment and marital satisfaction for young parents, prosocial behaviour in elementary school children).

Fathers in Families

The changing role of the father
in the family

Edited by
**Dorothea E. Dette-Hagenmeyer,
Andrea B. Erzinger and
Barbara Reichle**

Taylor & Francis Group

LONDON AND NEW YORK

First published 2016 by Routledge

2 Park Square, Milton Park, Abingdon, Oxon OX14 4RN
711 Third Avenue, New York, NY 10017, USA

Routledge is an imprint of the Taylor & Francis Group, an informa business

First issued in paperback 2017

British Library Cataloguing in Publication Data
A catalogue record for this book is available from the British Library

ISBN 13: 978-1-138-93547-1 (hbk)
ISBN 13: 978-1-138-09496-3 (pbk)

Typeset in Times New Roman
by RefineCatch Limited, Bungay, Suffolk

Publisher's Note
The publisher accepts responsibility for any inconsistencies that may have
arisen during the conversion of this book from journal articles to book chapters,
namely the possible inclusion of journal terminology.

Disclaimer
Every effort has been made to contact copyright holders for their permission to
reprint material in this book. The publishers would be grateful to hear from any
copyright holder who is not here acknowledged and will undertake to rectify
any errors or omissions in future editions of this book.

Contents

CONTENTS

Citation Information

The chapters in this book were originally published in the *European Journal of Developmental Psychology*, volume 11, issue 2 (March 2014). When citing this material, please use the original page numbering for each article, as follows:

Introduction

The changing role of the father in the family
Dorothea E. Dette-Hagenmeyer, Andrea B. Erzinger, and Barbara Reichle
European Journal of Developmental Psychology, volume 11, issue 2 (March 2014) pp. 129–135

Chapter 1

Family structure, maternal employment, and change in children's externalizing problem behaviour: Differences by age and self-regulation
Natasha J. Cabrera, Sandra L. Hofferth, and Gregory Hancock
European Journal of Developmental Psychology, volume 11, issue 2 (March 2014) pp. 136–158

Chapter 2

Predicting adolescents' parent–child relationship quality from parental personality, marital conflict and adolescents' personality
Harald Werneck, Maximilian Oscar Eder, Takuya Yanagida, and Brigitte Rollett
European Journal of Developmental Psychology, volume 11, issue 2 (March 2014) pp. 159–176

Chapter 3

Intergenerational transmission of maternal and paternal parenting beliefs: The moderating role of interaction quality
Andrea B. Erzinger and Andrea E. Steiger
European Journal of Developmental Psychology, volume 11, issue 2 (March 2014) pp. 177–195

CITATION INFORMATION

Chapter 4

Parents' depressive symptoms and children's adjustment over time are mediated by parenting, but differentially for fathers and mothers
Dorothea E. Dette-Hagenmeyer and Barbara Reichle
European Journal of Developmental Psychology, volume 11, issue 2 (March 2014) pp. 196–210

Chapter 5

Gender-specific macro- and micro-level processes in the transmission of gender role orientation in adolescence: The role of fathers
Markus Hess, Angela Ittel, and Aiden Sisler
European Journal of Developmental Psychology, volume 11, issue 2 (March 2014) pp. 211–226

Chapter 6

Effects of different facets of paternal and maternal control behaviour on early adolescents' perceived academic competence
Melanie Stutz and Beate Schwarz
European Journal of Developmental Psychology, volume 11, issue 2 (March 2014) pp. 227–241

Chapter 7

Couples' evaluations of fatherhood in different stages of the family life cycle
Franziska Fuhrmans, Holger von der Lippe, and Urs Fuhrer
European Journal of Developmental Psychology, volume 11, issue 2 (March 2014) pp. 242–258

Chapter 8

Paternal involvement elevates trajectories of life satisfaction during transition to parenthood
Alexandru Agache, Birgit Leyendecker, Esther Schäfermeier, and Axel Schölmerich
European Journal of Developmental Psychology, volume 11, issue 2 (March 2014) pp. 259–277

For any permission-related enquiries please visit:
http://www.tandfonline.com/page/help/permissions

Notes on Contributors

Alexandru Agache is based in the Department of Developmental Psychology, Ruhr-Universität Bochum, Germany.

Natasha J. Cabrera is Professor in the Department of Human Development and Quantitative Methodology, College of Education, at University of Maryland, College Park, MD, USA. Her research focuses on father involvement and children's social development, ethnic and cultural variations in fathering and mothering behaviors, family processes in a social and cultural context, and the mechanisms that link early experiences to children's school readiness.

Dorothea E. Dette-Hagenmeyer is a Research Associate in the Department of Psychology at the Ludwigsburg University of Education, Germany. She earned her Ph.D. from the Friedrich-Alexander-University Erlangen-Nuremberg, Germany. She conducted research into family (parenting, co-parenting, coping, close relationships), gender roles, work-life-balance, and evidence-based parenting programs and has a teaching record in research methods, developmental, social and positive psychology.

Maximilian Oscar Eder is an Assistant Professor in the Department of Applied Psychology at the University of Vienna, Austria.

Andrea B. Erzinger achieved a Master's Degree in Education, Private Law and Political Science at the University of Zurich, Switzerland, and is currently a research assistant at the University of Teacher Education (PHSG), St. Gallen, Switzerland. Her research interests are social and emotional development over the life course, familial intergenerational relationships, school-family-interaction and development of competencies.

Urs Fuhrer is a Professor in the Department of Psychology at Otto-von-Guericke-University, Magdeburg, Germany.

Franziska Fuhrmans is a Faculty Member in the Department of Psychology at Otto-von-Guericke-University, Magdeburg, Germany.

Gregory Hancock is a Professor in the Department of Human Development and Quantitative Methodology, College of Education, at University of Maryland, College Park, MD, USA.

Markus Hess is a Faculty Member in the Department of Education and Psychology at the Freie Universität Berlin, Germany.

Sandra L. Hofferth is a Professor in the Department of Family Science at the University of Maryland, College Park, MD, USA. Her research interests are in American children's use of time and later health outcomes, work and family, fathers and fathering, and family policy.

Angela Ittel is a Professor in the Institute of Education, and Vice-President of, the Technische Universität Berlin, Germany.

Birgit Leyendecker is Professor in the Department of Developmental Psychology, Ruhr-Universität Bochum, Germany.

Barbara Reichle is Professor of Developmental and Educational Psychology at Ludwigsburg University of Education, Germany. She completed a Doctoral degree in Psychology from Trier University, Germany. Her research focuses on the socio-emotional development of children within families and schools, parenting, intimate relationships, the transition to parenthood, and justice in the family. She is co-author of two evidence-based evaluated prevention programs (attachment and marital satisfaction for young parents, prosocial behaviour in elementary school children).

Brigitte Rollett is Professor Emeritus in the Department of Applied Psychology at the University of Vienna, Austria.

Esther Schäfermeier is Deputy Head of the Zentrum für Diagnostik und Förderung at the University of Cologne, Germany.

Axel Schölmerich is a Professor in the Department of Developmental Psychology at Ruhr-Universität Bochum, Germany.

Beate Schwarz is Professor of Psychology in the School of Applied Psychology at Zurich University of Applied Sciences, Winterthur, Switzerland.

Aiden Sisler is a Research Assistant in the Institute of Education at the Technische Universität Berlin, Germany.

Andrea E. Steiger is a post-doctoral researcher in the Institute of Psychology at the University of Zurich, Switzerland.

Melanie Stutz is based at the Swiss Coordination Centre for Research in Education, Aarau, Switzerland.

Holger von der Lippe is a Research Scientist in the Department of Psychology at Otto-von-Guericke-University, Magdeburg, Germany.

Harald Werneck is an Associate Professor in the Department of Applied Psychology at the University of Vienna, Austria.

Takuya Yanagida is a doctoral candidate in the Research Center Linz, University of Applied Sciences Upper Austria, Linz, Austria.

The changing role of the father in the family

Dorothea E. Dette-Hagenmeyer[1], Andrea B. Erzinger[2], and Barbara Reichle[1]

[1]Department of Psychology and Sociology, Ludwigsburg University of Education, Ludwigsburg, Germany
[2]Institute of Research on Teaching Profession and on Development of Competencies, University of Teacher Education St. Gallen, St. Gallen, Switzerland

The most universal property of a father is his *biological* (i.e., genetic) contribution to his children. Thus, fathers are indispensable for human reproduction. However, biologically speaking, the mother has more to invest than the father by enduring a long pregnancy, giving birth, and subsequently feeding and caring for the infant. After conception, the male is not needed anymore for the survival of the child if the mother is able to take care of herself or is cared for by others during pregnancy and childbed. Hence, fathers are much more biologically dispensable than mothers (see Werneck, 1998). After birth, the role of the mother is determined by the needs of the newborn—food and care. Support can come from the father or from others. Socially, however, humankind has developed many cultures and societies that include the father in the care of children and the family.

The form of this care, though, is not universally agreed upon but is instead largely defined by the respective culture. *Historically*, many forms of paternal care have been documented. In ancient Egypt, the father was a provider and an educator of the children. In ancient Greece, the role of the "head of the family" was more important as the father also had to provide for his family. In the monotheistic religion of Judaism, the father became important as an ancestor in the genealogical line of the family (see Werneck, 1998). *Anthropology* has identified substantial variation in the roles of fathers between cultures, ranging from the matrilineal extreme Mosuo (Na) culture in Himalayan China, which has been labelled a society without fathers (Hua, 2008), to egalitarian Qhawqhat Lahu (Du, 2000) and contemporary Western cultures with egalitarian tendencies, and finally to patriarchal cultures at the other extreme—"societies in which the

1

efficient performance of tasks that yield the most status and power is facilitated by men's size and strength and is in conflict with women's reproductive activities" (Wood & Eagly, 2002, p. 710).

Sociology has observed that patriarchal specialization tends to erode with the weakening of gender hierarchies in post-industrial societies (Wood & Eagly, 2002, p. 717): as the education of women, the quality of health care and the judicial equality of women and men increase, fertility rates decrease (Hobcraft, 1993). At the same time, female employment increases and brings with it the ability of women to self-support, and thus women's dependency on men as providers decreases. This gives more importance to notions of romantic love, mutual understanding and mutual support, all of which lead to the male having closer contact with his female partner during pregnancy and childbirth and even to subsequent hormonal changes in the father. These changes have been shown to increase paternal responsiveness to infant cries, which may help new fathers become attached to their newborns (see Storey, Walsh, Quinton, & Wynne-Edwards, 2000). We therefore expect that qualitative differences in enacting the role of the father versus the mother will be more pointed in cultures and subcultures that are more patriarchally oriented and allow for less role flexibility. In such (sub)cultures, traditional male versus female role enactments (e.g., rough and tumble play in fathers, sports and instrumental activities, disciplining) should be more frequently observed. An example is a subcultural variation in the use of paternal parental leave in Sweden. When their partners stay home with the infant, Swedish mothers usually join the workforce, whereas immigrant mothers stay home. Swedish fathers who stay home with the infant perform all kinds of household chores, but immigrant fathers are not involved in household chores (Chronholm, 2002).

Research on fathers began with a strong focus on the impact of the father on child development in the late 1960s and early 1970s, triggered by a growing interest in the *effects of father absence*. On sociological grounds, moral guidance, breadwinning, gender-role modelling especially in boys, marital support and nurturance have been identified as *specific facets of the father role* (for overviews, see Lamb, 2000; Paquette, Coyl-Shepherd, & Newland, 2013). In the 1990s, fundamental shifts in family life, increasing rates of mothers in the paid labour force, as well as changes in gender roles led to fundamental changes in social policy. As a consequence, a growing body of research has emphasized the role of fathers in families (Cabrera, Tamis-LeMonda, Bradley, Hofferth, & Lamb, 2000; Marsiglio, Amato, Day, & Lamb, 2000). Increasing divorce rates and single parenthood triggered public interest in fatherhood and the father's contribution to family life and child development (Marsiglio et al., 2000). Thus, after much research on the absence of fathers, research on the importance of fathers and their contributions to child development increased.

In recent years, research has identified fathers as *providers of material, emotional or informational support* to children and mothers. Along these

2

dimensions, paternal involvement has been investigated in terms of fathers' accessibility (e.g., their presence and availability, their engagement in play and other activities with the child, as well as their responsibility for decision-making with regard to childcare and practical issues; Lamb, Pleck, Charnov, & Levine, 1987; Parke, 2013a). With regard to fathers' accessibility, most studies have considered the father's cohabitation with the mother to be an indicator of paternal involvement (Sarkadi, Kristiansson, Oberklaid, & Bremberg, 2008). Overall and with few exceptions, the cohabitation of fathers and mothers seems to reduce behavioural problems in children (Carlson, 2006; Flouri & Buchanan, 2002; Vaden-Kiernan, Ialongo, Pearson, & Kellam, 1995). Paternal engagement has been shown to positively affect the social, behavioural, psychological and cognitive outcomes of children (Cabrera & Tamis-LeMonda, 2013; Sarkadi et al., 2008). Referring to fathers' responsibility, a majority of studies have focused on the financial support fathers provide and have underlined the importance of fathers as financial suppliers of their families for the well-being of children and mothers (Sigle-Rushton & McLanahan, 2004). Most research in this field has found that paternal involvement is influential for children's well-being, and only a minority of studies have found no effect of father involvement, particularly after controlling for socio-economic factors (Crockett, Eggebeen, & Hawkins, 1993).

Besides the specific facets of father involvement that affect child development, another focus lies on the *specific developmental domains influenced by fathers*. Father involvement has been found to contribute importantly to children's cognitive (McWayne, Downer, Campos, & Harris, 2013) and social development (Leidy, Schofield, & Parke, 2013). As shown by a review of longitudinal studies in this field, children who lived with their mother and her male partner exhibited fewer externalizing problem behaviours. Furthermore, engaging with the child regularly and in an active way has been longitudinally associated with positive child outcomes such as educational attainment (Flouri & Buchanan, 2004). Father involvement was found to promote children's cognitive development by constraining the negative impact of low family SES (Sarkadi et al., 2008). On the other hand, the involvement of fathers who do not reside with the mothers—particularly involvement in child-related activities, having productive father–child relationships and engaging with the child—had significant positive effects on children's social and emotional well-being, academic achievement and behavioural adjustment. Surprisingly, no significant effects on children's well-being have been identified by the amount of father–child contact or fathers' financial contributions (Adamsons & Johnson, 2013).

Another strong focus of research has been on the *specific processes by which fathers shape their children's development*. In the traditional family, in addition to the emotional baseline that mothers provide, fathers have been viewed as enforcers of discipline and child compliance. In a later stage, they were viewed as the suppliers of financial support as well as important gender-role models (Pleck & Pleck, 2010). Hence, for a long time, parenting in terms of nurturing and guiding children through their development seemed to be a maternal task, with research focusing on mother–child dyads. Additional data were collected from teachers rather than from fathers. Meanwhile, several longitudinal studies have contrasted fathering from mothering and discussed the long-term implications of their different impacts (for an overview, see Sarkadi et al., 2008).

The *aim of this special issue* is to highlight the role of fathers in the family by presenting eight longitudinal studies from various Western countries. Six studies focus on socialization outcomes in children or adolescents, two studies predict parents' satisfaction. As we are convinced that in order to capture the complex interplay within a family and to point out the properties or effects of fathers in this context requires comparisons between mothers and fathers, all of these studies compare mothers and fathers to investigate differences. Within a socialization model such as Bronfenbrenner's (1994) ecosystemic model, socialization means complex interactions between (1) the child as a developing person with specific characteristics in (2) a specific developmental context with (2.1) physical and social properties and (2.2) the father and the mother as socialization agents with (2.2.1) specific characteristics and (2.2.2) behaviours to (3) produce specific developmental outcomes.

Cabrera, Hofferth, and Hancock as well as Werneck, Eder, Yanagida, and Rollett analysed (2.1) the social conditions of child development. Cabrera et al. studied the effects of two different social conditions, that is mothers' employment and living with a biological father or stepfather in early childhood at age of four on the socioemotional behaviour of the child. Werneck et al. focused on another social condition, which is the presence or absence of marital conflict in children's families and the relations between conflict and adolescents' personality and parent–child relationships. Erzinger and Steiger, Dette-Hagenmeyer and Reichle, Hess, Ittel, and Sisler, and Werneck et al. analysed (2.2.1) variation in the traits of the socialization agents: the father's personality, values, beliefs, health, etc. and their relations with child development. Erzinger and Steiger focused on the intergenerational transmission of harsh parenting beliefs across 23 years. Dette-Hagenmeyer and Reichle studied the relations between maternal and paternal depressive symptoms and the sociobehavioural development of children. Hess et al. investigated the transmission of gender-role orientations from fathers and mothers to adolescent children. Werneck et al. analysed relations between maternal and paternal personality and adolescents' parent–child relationships, as well as personality.

Specific socialization behaviours (2.2.2) of the parents as socialization agents were investigated by several studies. Dette-Hagenmeyer and Reichle studied the relations between positive parenting, inconsistent discipline, parental depression and the socioemotional development of the child. Hess et al. analysed the relations between gender-specific parenting and gender-role orientations. Stutz and Schwarz focused on the relations between mothers' and fathers' monitoring and authoritarian control and adolescents' engagement in school and academic competence.

Two papers focused on the relations between the socialization agents (i.e., mothers and fathers) over the course of enacting their roles. Fuhrmans, von der Lippe and Fuhrer studied paternal competences and parents as well as their spouses' satisfaction with role enactment. Agache, Leyendecker, Schäfermeier and Schölmerich compared the life satisfaction trajectories of mothers and fathers around the birth of a child and studied relations between fathers' involvement in childcare and housework and mothers' satisfaction.

Finally, several papers also analysed moderating and mediating processes in the family systems: parenting was studied as a mediator between parental depression and child problem behaviour (Dette-Hagenmeyer & Reichle) as well as between the gender-role orientations of parents and children (Hess et al.), adolescents' engagement in school was studied as a mediator between monitoring and authoritarian control and adolescents' perceived academic competence (Stutz & Schwarz), fathers' involvement was studied as a moderator of mothers' changes in life satisfaction (Agache et al.), children's capacity to self-regulate was studied as a moderator of the relation between stepfather cohabitation and subsequent reductions in externalizing behaviour (Cabrera et al.) and parent–child interaction quality was studied as a moderator of the transmission of harsh parenting beliefs to the next generation (Erzinger & Steiger).

So what is special about fathers, and what is not? In their conjugal relationships, fathers have an influence on the well-being of their spouses by means of their share of childcare and housework around the time of childbirth, although this comes at a partial cost (Agache et al.). Fathers contribute to mothers' satisfaction by interacting with children and contributing to childcare; however, this can instigate maternal gatekeeping (Fuhrmans et al.). It would be interesting to know whether such negative side effects of paternal involvement disappear when the quality of paternal involvement meets their spouses' quality standards—i.e., whether it is a function of quality or competition, similar to male gatekeeping in the professional world. In sum, mothers seem to be supported and relieved by a more egalitarian distribution of childcare. We do not know, however, whether this extends to the facets of fathers' traditional roles (e.g., material support of the family) and whether fathers feel a similar degree of support and relief from a more egalitarian distribution of traditional father roles.

With respect to the socialization of children, the presence of fathers and stepfathers is superior to their absence (Cabrera et al.). Fathers' impact on the academic development of their children (Stutz & Schwarz), on the socio-emotional development of their children (Dette-Hagenmeyer & Reichle), on the parenting beliefs of their children (Erzinger & Steiger), on the gender-role orientation of their children (Hess et al.) and on the quality of their relationships with their adolescent children (Werneck et al.) are similar to the impact of mothers. Our studies show how fathers matter and that they matter in ways that are similar to the ways in which mothers matter, a finding that reflects the more egalitarian stage of family development in the cultures that were studied (Austria, Germany, Switzerland and the USA).

However, some effects have been found to be less pointed in fathers than in mothers, reflecting fathers' lower involvement with their children, or to work in a different way for fathers, reflecting the traditional roles and distributions. Fathers seem to be less able to immunize their parenting against depressive tendencies (Dette-Hagenmeyer & Reichle), they monitor their children significantly less than mothers (Stutz & Schwarz), their marital conflict behaviour impacts the adolescent–parent relationship (Werneck et al), their interaction quality with the children does not moderate the transmission of harsh parenting beliefs to their children (Erzinger & Steiger), but the transmission of their gender-role orientations to their offspring is mediated by their gender-specific parenting (Hess et al.).

These differences might reflect not only the different quality of fathers' involvement with their children (i.e., smaller time segments due to longer employment hours, or more leisure time activities as compared to mothers who have to align their interactions with the child with housework, errands and the like), but also more of the classical paternal attitude, or simply lower competence standards or levels. Comparisons between same-sex parents and heterosexual parents could help to disentangle the effects of sex and gender. Thus, this impact of fathers on children, on mothers and on the familial interplay with regard to positive family development should be explored with more moderating and mediating variables. It should also be endorsed by further research on families in other cultures and new types of families within our own culture—such as families with same-sex parents, patchwork families, and families with extrafamilial paternal and maternal figures, just to name a few (see also Parke, 2013b). And such research should result in the adaptation of our theories to the constantly changing concept of fatherhood.

REFERENCES

Adamsons, K., & Johnson, S. K. (2013). An updated and expanded meta-analysis of nonresident fathering and child well-being. *Journal of Family Psychology, 27,* 589–599.

Bronfenbrenner, U. (1994). Ecological models of human development. In T. Husen & T. N. Postlethwaite (Eds.), *International encyclopedia of education* (2nd ed., vol. 3, pp. 1643–1647). Oxford: Pergamon.

Cabrera, N. J., & Tamis-LeMonda, C. S. (Eds.). (2013). *Handbook of father involvement: Multidisciplinary perspectives* (2nd ed.). London: Routledge.

Cabrera, N. J., Tamis-LeMonda, C. S., Bradley, R., Hofferth, S., & Lamb, M. E. (2000). Fatherhood in the twenty-first century. *Child Development, 71,* 127–136.

Carlson, M. J. (2006). Family structure, father involvement, and adolescent behavioral outcomes. *Journal of Marriage and Family, 68,* 137–154.

Chronholm, A. (2002). Which fathers use their rights? Swedish fathers who take parental leave. *Community, Work & Family, 5,* 365–370.

Crockett, L. J., Eggebeen, D. J., & Hawkins, A. J. (1993). Father's presence and young children's behavioral and cognitive adjustment. *Journal of Family Issues, 14,* 355–377.

Du, S. (2000). 'Husband and wife do it together': Sex/gender allocation of labor among the Qhawqhat Lahu of Lancang, Southwest China. *American Anthropologist, 102,* 520–537.

Flouri, E., & Buchanan, A. (2002). What predicts good relationships with parents in adolescence and partners in adult life: Findings from the 1958 British Birth Cohort. *Journal of Family Psychology, 16,* 186–198.

Flouri, E., & Buchanan, A. (2004). Early father's and mother's involvement and child's later educational outcomes. *British Journal of Educational Psychology, 74,* 141–153.

Hobcraft, J. (1993). Women's education, child welfare and child survival: A review of the evidence. *Health Transition Review, 3,* 159–173.

Hua, C. (2008). *A society without fathers or husbands: The Na of China* (2nd ed.). Brooklyn, NY: Zone Books.

Lamb, M. E. (2000). The history of research on fathers involvement: An overview. *Marriage and Family Review, 29,* 23–42.

Lamb, M. E., Pleck, J. H., Charnov, E., & Levine, J. (1987). A biological perspective on paternal behavior and involvement. In J. Lancaster, J. Altmann, A. Rossi, & L. Sherrod (Eds.), *Foundations of human behavior: Parenting across the life span: Biosocial dimensions* (pp. 111–142). New York, NY: Aldine de Gruyter.

Leidy, M. S., Schofield, T. J., & Parke, R. D. (2013). Fathers' contributions to children social development. In N. J. Cabrera & C. S. Tamis-LeMonda (Eds.), *Handbook of father involvement: Multidisciplinary perspectives* (2nd ed., pp. 151–167). London: Routledge.

Marsiglio, W., Amato, P. R., Day, R. D., & Lamb, M. E. (2000). Scholarship on fatherhood in the 1990s and beyond. *Journal of Marriage and Family, 62,* 1173–1191.

McWayne, C., Downer, J. T., Campos, R., & Harris, R. D. (2013). Father involvement during early childhood and its association with children's early learning: A meta-analysis. *Early Education and Development, 24,* 898–922.

Paquette, D., Coyl-Shepherd, D. D., & Newland, L. A. (2013). Fathers and development: New areas for exploration. *Early Child Development and Care, 183,* 735–745.

Parke, R. D. (2013a). Gender differences and similarities in parenting. In K. K. Kline & W. B. Wilcox (Eds.), *Gender and parenthood: Natural and social scientific perspectives* (pp. 120–163). New York, NY: Columbia University Press.

Parke, R. D. (2013b). *Future families.* Chichester: Wiley-Blackwell.

Pleck, E., & Pleck, J. (2010). Fatherhood ideals in the United States: Historical dimensions. In M. E. Lamb (Ed.), *The role of the father in child development* (5th ed., pp. 33–48). Hoboken, NJ: Wiley.

Sarkadi, A., Kristiansson, R., Oberklaid, F., & Bremberg, S. (2008). Fathers' involvement and children's developmental outcomes: A systematic review of longitudinal studies. *Acta Paediatrica, 97,* 153–158.

Sigle-Rushton, W., & McLanahan, S. (2004). Father-absence and child well-being: A critical review. In D. Moynihan, T. Smeeding, & L. Rainwater (Eds.), *The future of the family* (pp. 116–155). New York, NY: Russell Sage.

Storey, A. E., Walsh, C. J., Quinton, R. L., & Wynne-Edwards, K. E. (2000). Hormonal correlates of paternal responsiveness in new and expectant fathers. *Evolution and Human Behavior, 21,* 79–95.

Vaden-Kiernan, N., Ialongo, N. S., Pearson, J., & Kellam, S. (1995). Household family structure and children's aggressive behavior: A longitudinal study of urban elementary school children. *Journal of Abnormal Child Psychology, 23,* 553–568.

Werneck, H. (1998). *Übergang zur Vaterschaft* [Transition to fatherhood]. Wien: Springer.

Wood, W., & Eagly, A. H. (2002). A cross-cultural analysis of the behavior of women and men: Implications for the origins of sex differences. *Psychological Bulletin, 128,* 699–727.

Family structure, maternal employment, and change in children's externalizing problem behaviour: Differences by age and self-regulation

Natasha J. Cabrera, Sandra L. Hofferth, and Gregory Hancock

Human Development and Quantitative Methodology, University of Maryland, College Park, MD, USA

This study used a latent difference score growth model to investigate how changes in family structure (biological father and stepfather residence) and maternal employment are associated with American children's externalizing problem behaviours (EPB) from ages 4–10 and whether these associations vary by children's level of self-regulation. For all 4-year-old children, living with a biological father at age 4 was associated with reductions in EPB at ages 4–6 and later years, with no variation by child self-regulation. Living with a stepfather at age 4 was associated with higher levels of EPB at age 4; however, for less-regulated children, stepfather residence at ages 4 and 8 was associated with reductions in EPB between ages 4–6 and 8–10, respectively. Greater employment hours were associated with increased EPB in the next 2 years for less-regulated children of all ages; however, except for the age 4–6 transition, there was a lagged association that reduced behaviour problems after 2 years and outweighed short-term increases.

Research on American school-age children and adolescents shows increased levels of externalizing problem behaviour (EPB) from low levels in the 1970s to high levels in 1999 (Achenbach, Dumenci, & Rescorla, 2003; Collishaw, Gardner, Maughan, Scott, & Pickles, 2012). These rates are alarming, given that EPB is the most common and persistent form of childhood maladjustment with long-term lasting effects (Campbell, 1995; Campbell, Shaw, & Gilliom, 2000). Although the causes of this increase include multiple individual and family-level factors, the centrality of the home in children's development is undisputable. The psychological literature has rightly focused on the parent–child relationship as an important contributor to children's behaviour. Other aspects of the home have received less attention in the psychological literature, but have emerged in the sociological literature as important influences on US children's development, namely maternal employment and family structure (e.g., father/stepfather residence). Recently, these aspects of family life have undergone dramatic shifts. From the 1970s to 1990s, the labor force participation of married mothers with a preschool age child increased from 37% in 1975 to 62% in 2009 and the proportion of children living with a biological mother and father declined from 77% in 1980 to 59% in 2010 (U.S. Census Bureau, 2012). These family structure changes (e.g., fathers exit or step fathers enter the family) as well as changes in maternal employment are important to consider in understanding changes in children's behaviours because they are likely to reduce the amount and quality of time parents have with their children, which may disrupt behaviour especially for children with limited regulatory skills (Bachman, Coley, & Carrano, 2011; Grusec, 2011; Rubin, Burgess, Dwyer, & Hastings, 2003).

Research linking family structure and maternal employment to children's EPB is limited in several ways. First, research on maternal employment focuses on the first years of life and pays less attention to the later childhood period (Han, Waldfogel, & Brooks-Gunn, 2001). Second, although research has shown that father residence in early childhood is linked to children's adjustment in adolescence (Cabrera, Cook, McFadden, & Bradley, 2012), less is known about how father residence might be linked to children's EPB across the early childhood period, especially during transitional periods which represent change and turmoil for some children (Cavanagh & Huston, 2008). Family changes might be especially trying during transitions into middle childhood or adolescence (Bachman et al., 2011; Cavanagh & Huston, 2008). Third, it is unclear how the entry of a stepfather influences children's behaviour across early childhood. Fourth, children's ability to cope with change in light of their self-regulatory behaviours has not been considered in past research (Cummings, El-Sheikh, Kouros, & Buckhalt, 2009). To address these gaps, we use data from the 1979 National Longitudinal Survey of Youth (NLSY79) (Center for Human Resource Research, 2004) to seek answers for the following questions: (1) are father/stepfather residence, maternal employment and child's self-regulation associated with children's EPB at age 4; (2) are father/stepfather residence and maternal employment associated with change in children's EPB differently across ages 4–10 and (3) does the association between father/stepfather residence and maternal employment and change in EPB vary by children's level of self-regulation?

CHANGES IN CHILDREN'S EPB

Externalizing behaviours, normative among toddlers, decline with age. As children get older, they are able to regulate their emotions and communicate their feelings with others. By school entry, most children (more than 70% by some national estimates) are age-appropriately compliant, prosocial and cooperative; only a small proportion (12% by some accounts) continues to show antisocial behaviours (NICHD Early Childcare Research Network, 2004).

CONTRIBUTION OF FAMILY STRUCTURE TO CHANGES IN EPB

We frame this paper using resource theory that parents with more resources (e.g., human capital, including education and income) are able to invest more in their children (e.g., providing cognitively stimulating experiences) than those with fewer resources (Haveman & Wolfe, 1994). Thus, children living in two-parent households are likely to have access to more resources, including parental time and stimulating experiences, than those who live with just one parent. Moreover, living in two-parent households with one's biological father can facilitate father–child interactions, which have been shown to be linked to children's social competence (Cabrera, Shannon, & Tamis-LeMonda, 2007; Tamis-LeMonda, Shannon, Cabrera, & Lamb, 2004). Not only are children living with just their mothers less likely to interact with their biological fathers, but they are also more likely to experience a new father figure, which might be beneficial (e.g., bringing additional resources to the household) or detrimental (e.g., creating emotional upheaval) (Amato, 1993).

Research in the last decade has shown that children who grow up living with both parents are less likely to exhibit EPB than children who do not (Hetherington & Stanley-Hagan, 1995; Hofferth, 2006). Magnuson and Berger (2009) found that children living in single-mother and social-father families exhibited increased behaviour problems over time, although another study found this association to be stronger for white than black children (Fomby & Cherlin, 2007). There is also evidence that changes in family structure are positively associated with behavioural problems (Osborne & McLanahan, 2007). Also, a recent study found that compared to children who did not reside with their fathers, children who resided with them in early childhood reported having a better father–child relationship, which was predictive of fewer EPB in adolescence (Cabrera et al., 2012).

However, studies to date have utilized an aggregate measure of father involvement—the proportion of time in a two biological parent family—which can underestimate the effect because it cannot ascertain that the EPB was related to particular transition of interest (e.g., entry of a stepfather) that may have occurred years before the EPB was assessed (Fomby & Cherlin, 2007; Magnuson & Berger, 2009; Osborne & McLanahan, 2007). Additionally, current methods cannot detect sleeper effects; that is, changes in behaviour may show up several years later. For example, instability in early childhood has been linked with outcomes in middle childhood (Cavanagh & Huston, 2008). In this study, we improve on past studies by including a measure of behaviour soon after the family changes and by examining delayed associations.

CONTRIBUTION OF MATERNAL EMPLOYMENT TO CHANGES IN EPB

Maternal employment can increase resources to the family and reduce maternal stress and hence improve parenting and reduce child EPB. But, it can also reduce the available time mothers have to spend with their children, which may lead to an increase in EPB. Research has shown that maternal employment has a positive influence on children's behaviour, but after the child's first year (Han et al., 2001). Because mothers fit their employment around their child's schedule (Sayer, Bianchi, & Robinson, 2004), the income gained may offset much of the potential negative impact on children (Coley et al., 2007). However, older children may demand more time and attention from their parents than younger children, and thus it is possible that maternal employment may influence children differently across the early childhood period. Mothers with long hours of work might be more fatigued and less able to monitor their preschool children's needs and behaviours than mothers who work fewer hours. One study found that fluctuating hours or unstable work was associated with children's EPB (Johnson, Kalil, & Dunifon, 2012). These findings suggest that it is important to examine not just the short-term but also the long-term association of employment and children's EPB at different ages, especially during the transition to formal school and into adolescence when children's needs might be heightened and place more demands on parents.

CONTRIBUTION OF CHILDREN'S SELF-REGULATION TO CHANGES IN EPB: MAIN AND MODERATING EFFECTS

The variability observed in EPB might also be related to differences in children's self-regulation, defined as the ability to manage one's behaviour, emotions and attention voluntarily and adaptively (Rothbart, Sheese, & Posner, 2007). Regulated children are able to control emotions and can relax, focus and enjoy social interactions. Self-regulation is commonly assessed with maternal reports of children's demandingness, soothability and distress in a novel situation. A consistent finding is that as children get older, they should be able to self-regulate and when they do not they are more likely to exhibit more EPB (Burgess, Marshall, Rubin, & Fox, 2003; Leve, Kim, & Pears, 2005). Less-regulated children are also more likely to be influenced by negative parenting than more regulated children (Larsson, Viding, Rijsdijk, & Plomin, 2008). A study found that 4 year olds who showed early dysregulated behaviours were more likely to exhibit externalizing problems when they experienced maternal negativity at age 4 than better regulated children (Rubin et al., 2003). It is likely then that children who are less regulated may have a difficult time dealing with new situations, especially when it results in fathers moving out of the house, a new stepfather moving in or mothers working longer hours.

HYPOTHESES

We examine the influence of the timing of father residence, stepfather residence and maternal employment on initial level of EPB at age 4 and then changes in EPB from ages 4 to 10. We test the following hypotheses: (1) children who reside with a biological father, who do not reside with a stepfather, who have a mother working fewer hours and who are self-regulated will exhibit lower levels of EPB at age 4 than their counterparts; (2) children who do not live with their biological fathers, who live with a stepfather and who have mothers who work more hours at age 4 are more likely to exhibit increased EPB over the following 2 years than children who experience no such changes, especially during transition periods; and (3) children who have low levels of self-regulation will exhibit more EPB when a father moves out, a new stepfather moves in or mothers work longer hours than children who are more regulated. We control throughout for the following individual and family variables because they are linked to EPB: child gender and language ability, family income and size, and maternal education, drug and alcohol use, and harsh parenting.

METHODS

Data: NLSY79

This analysis uses data on the children of female youth interviewed as part of the NLSY79, which obtained detailed information on the children from the mother every other year beginning in 1986. We used information from the 1988 through 2004 waves to measure the behaviour and family circumstances of birth cohorts of children at ages 4, 6, 8 and 10.

Exclusions. To have complete data for all children, we excluded children who did not have self-regulation data. Identical analyses of the complete sample of 9324 and of the final sample of 4967 produced the same results, indicating no systematic bias. The sample was weighted using customized weights from the NLSY79, so the results are representative of the children born in 1979 to American women between the ages of 14 and 21.

Measures: Dependent variable

Children's EPB were measured using the Behaviour Problems Index, a parent-reported measure of the incidence and severity of child EPB using items originally drawn from the Achenbach scale (Achenbach et al., 2003) and validated for use in the NLSY79. The present study focused on the subset of 11 items identified by the NLSY79 as assessing EPB ($\alpha = .81$). Indicators, coded as $1 = $ not true, $2 = $ sometimes true, $3 = $ often true, include the following: moody, high strung, cheats, argues, bullies, disobeys, does not get along, not liked, irritable, has a temper and breaks things. The total score for each age is the sum of these 11 items.

Independent variables

Residential biological father is based on the maternal report of whether the child's biological father was present in the household at each wave ($1 = $ yes, $0 = $ no). If the biological father was not in the household and the mother reported that her husband/partner lived in the household, then *residential stepfather* was coded 1, otherwise it was coded 0. Because father behaviour was not a focus of the early years of the mother–child supplement to the NLSY79, father and stepfather residence in the household up to age 10 are the only measures of father involvement available.

Maternal employment at child ages 4, 6, 8 and 10 was defined as the average number of hours per week worked since the last interview 2 years earlier.

Child self-regulation was assessed in the year the child was 4 years old by using three mother-report indicators ($\alpha = .57$): (1) Soothability: How often does the mother have trouble soothing the child when upset; (2) Distress: When you leave the room and leave the child alone, how often does she/he get upset; and (3) Demandingness: How often is the child demanding and impatient even when you are busy. Each of these variables was coded on a 5-point scale: $1 = $ almost never, $2 = $ less than half the time, $3 = $ about half the time, $4 = $ more than half the time and $5 = $ always. Higher scores indicate that the child has a lower degree of self-regulation. Confirmatory factor analysis was used to evaluate the measurement of this latent construct.

Control variables

The *gender of the child* ($1 = $ female, $0 = $ male) was measured using the 2004 survey wave. *Children's language ability* was assessed using the total raw scores on the Peabody Picture Vocabulary Test-Revised Form L (PPVT) for the year the child was 4 years old. *Family income* (natural log) was taken when the child was 4, 6, 8 and 10 from key variables in NLSY79 (total net pre-tax family income from last calendar year, truncated). The *total number of children in the household* was the sum of biological, adopted, step and foster children assessed when the child's age was 4, 6, 8 and 10.

Harsh parenting was measured when the child was 4 years of age. The mother was asked what her response would be if her child hit her. If she responded that she would either hit the child back or spank the child, then it was coded as harsh parenting (1); if she reported that she would send child to room, talk to child, ignore child or give child a chore, then it was coded as non-harsh parenting (0).

Maternal education is a continuous measure of the highest grade the mother completed by the interview when the child was age 4 (1 = 1st grade through 20 = 8th year of college or more).

Maternal drug and alcohol use was assessed regularly but inconsistently across waves in the NLSY79. Mother's ever use of drugs up to when the child was age 4 (0 = no drugs, 1 = one drug only and 2 = two drugs) was created from questions asking about marijuana and cocaine/crack cocaine use. Maternal alcohol use when the child was 4 was measured by the number of days the mother reporting drinking alcohol in the last month.

Analytic plan

The 4-, 6-, 8- and 10-year measures of EPB were modelled using a latent difference score model (McArdle & Hamagami, 2001). Although one could proceed in two phases (unconditional growth model and then a conditional growth model), we elected to proceed directly to the conditional model given the theoretical rationale for the covariate. As shown in Figure 1, latent variables (circles) were constructed so as to represent the intercept (EPB at age 4) and changes in EPB from years 4 to 6, 6 to 8 and 8 to 10. The observed outcomes (rectangles) were the sum of the intercept and change in EPB in all temporally preceding adjacent pairs of latent variables. The covariates were self-regulation (latent in the first model and observed when examining group differences) and the family environment variables (observed)—father residence, stepfather residence and maternal employment at age 4, 6, 8 and 10. Time-dependent covariates (family income and number of children at each age) and time-independent covariates (e.g., gender) were included in the models, as appropriate. Residuals of the latent difference portion of the model were also allowed to covary above and beyond the covariates' influences.

Modelling was conducted using the EQS 6.1 structural equation modelling software with missing data estimated by full information maximum likelihood (FIML). Model fit was evaluated using the comparative fit index (CFI) and the root mean square error of approximation (RMSEA).

Based on children's self-regulation scores (range 1–15), 1324 children in the upper quartile with scores from 7 to 15 were assigned to the "low regulation" group and 3643 children in the lower three-quarters of the distribution with scores from 1 to 6 were assigned to the "high regulation" group. The conclusions of the study were not sensitive to the cut point. To test the overall hypothesis of differences in the models for the two self-regulation groups, we computed the chi-square statistic for a model with all parameters constrained to be equal across groups and for a model without these constraints. Chi-square change ($\Delta\chi^2$) was used to assess statistical significance. We used the same strategy to test for

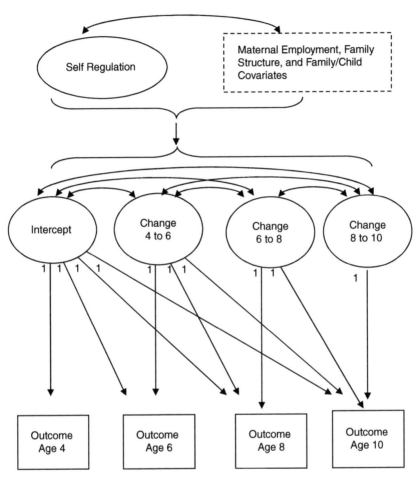

Figure 1. Latent difference score model, with covariates.

similarity of sets of coefficients. Effect sizes were calculated by dividing significant unstandardized coefficients by the standard deviation of age-specific externalizing behaviour.

RESULTS

Descriptive analyses

Based on the unconditional means, average levels of EPB were stable from ages 4 to 10 (Table 1). Other variables displayed expected trends over time. Maternal weekly work hours increased from 15 at age 4 to 20.9 at age 8. Sixty-nine percent of children were living with a residential father at age 8, compared with 76% at age 4; the proportion of children living with a stepfather increased from 7% at age 4 to 10% at age 8. Family income and family size remained relatively constant. On average, mothers had completed 13 years of schooling when the child was age 4.

Children in our sample averaged 5.3 out of 15 on the self-regulation scale (assessed as the sum of three indicators: trouble soothing, gets upset, and demanding), suggesting moderate levels of self-regulation. Less regulated 4-year-old children were reported to have higher levels of EPB (2.32 points more) than those who were more self-regulated (Table 1). The results were

TABLE 1
Weighted means, proportions, and standard deviations

Variable description	Full sample		More self-regulated		Less self-regulated		t-Test
	Mean	SD	Mean	SD	Mean	SD	Significance[a]
Externalizing (4)	15.24	3.42	14.78	3.14	17.10	3.87	<.001
Externalizing (6)	15.23	3.54	14.95	3.40	16.66	4.00	<.001
Externalizing (8)	15.31	3.62	15.08	3.53	16.59	4.07	<.001
Externalizing (10)	15.24	3.64	15.09	3.56	16.33	3.96	<.001
Mother's education	13.00	2.38	12.78	2.40	12.00	2.32	<.001
Female	0.49	0.50	0.50	0.50	0.50	0.50	ns
Trouble soothing	1.62	0.99					
Gets upset	1.40	0.85					
Demanding	2.54	1.16					
Low self-regulation	5.31	2.40					
PPVT	48.61	18.21	45.85	18.67	39.91	17.74	<.001
Alcohol	3.78	4.91	3.52	4.64	3.44	4.86	ns
Drug use	0.60	0.49	0.56	0.50	0.52	0.50	ns
Harsh parenting	0.43	0.50	0.49	0.50	0.55	0.50	<.05
Maternal work hours (4)	15.05	14.57	14.45	14.00	13.93	14.47	ns
Maternal work hours (6)	18.03	16.05	17.19	15.48	16.70	15.98	ns
Maternal work hours (8)	20.94	17.00	20.53	16.74	20.26	17.52	ns
Family income (4)	10.36	0.99	10.22	0.98	9.92	1.06	<.001
Family income (6)	10.45	1.04	10.33	0.98	10.00	1.08	<.001
Family income (8)	10.51	1.03	10.39	1.00	10.09	1.08	<.001
Residential father (4)	0.76	0.43	0.71	0.45	0.61	0.49	<.001
Residential father (6)	0.72	0.45	0.68	0.47	0.56	0.50	<.001
Residential father (8)	0.69	0.46	0.64	0.48	0.54	0.50	<.001
Stepfather (4)	0.07	0.26	0.09	0.29	0.06	0.24	ns
Stepfather (6)	0.08	0.27	0.09	0.28	0.10	0.29	<.05
Stepfather (8)	0.10	0.30	0.10	0.30	0.10	0.30	ns
Number of children (4)	2.30	1.09	2.40	1.14	2.39	1.25	ns
Number of children (6)	2.35	1.15	2.48	1.18	2.42	1.28	ns
Number of children (8)	2.39	1.19	2.52	1.23	2.39	1.32	<.05
N	4967		3643		1324		

[a] Result of a t-test comparing children who are more self-regulated with those who are less self-regulated.

similar at ages 6, 8 and 10, though the difference declined over time. The EPB of self-regulated children remained stable over ages 4–10, (14.78–15.09), whereas those of less regulated children declined, from 17.10 to 16.33.

Fewer less-regulated children were living with a residential father at age 4 and at later ages than more regulated children; only residence with a stepfather at age 6 differed by level of self-regulation.

Measurement model

The confirmatory factor analysis of the indicators of low self-regulation for the full sample shows that the model fits the data with a CFI of .999 (Table 2). "Child is demanding" and "gets upset when left" are the items most closely linked to the construct of self-regulation and "trouble soothing" is the item least linked. In this study, the construct of self-regulation measures the ability of the child to inhibit responses and control his/her emotions.

EPB—Full sample

The overall fit for the full sample model was excellent, with a CFI of .995 and an RMSEA of .028 with a 90% confidence interval of .025 to .031.

EPB at age 4. Examining the structural model of EPB at age 4 (the Intercept column in Table 3), the variables included in the model explain 42% of the variance in externalizing behaviour at age 4 because of the strong contribution of low self-regulation. With poorer self-regulation, mothers reported increased child EPB.

At age 4, biological father residence was not related to EPB. Children living with a stepfather exhibited significantly higher EPB, controlling for level of self-regulation and other variables. Maternal work hours were not related to the child's EPB in the full sample. Results for control variables are presented in the tables but not described in the text.

Change in EPB from age 4 to 6. Children living with a biological father at age 4 showed a greater decline in EPB from age 4 to 6 than those not living with their biological father at age 4. Compared to more regulated children, less regulated

TABLE 2
Measurement model

Self-regulation	Standardized loading
Trouble soothing child	0.388
Child gets upset when left	0.576
Child is demanding	0.634
N	4967

$\chi^2 = 766.757$, 3 df, $p < .001$
CFI = .999; reliability coefficient rho = .567

TABLE 3

Coefficients from the structural model of parent involvement, full sample ($N = 4967$)

Variable description	A Intercept			B Change age 4–6			C Change age 6–8			D Change age 8–10		
	β	b	SE	β	b	SE	β	b	SE	β	b	SE
Mother's education	.004	.006	.026	−.040*	−.050	.023	−.010	−.013	.024	.007	.008	.028
Child female	−.039*	−.264	.103	−.020	−.116	.092	−.022	−.129	.094	.027	.149	.082
Child PPVT score	.051*	.010	.004	.006	.001	.004	.012	.002	.004	−.015	−.002	.004
Alcohol	.025	.017	.012	.017	.010	.011	−.011	−.006	.012	.048*	.027	.011
Drug use	.034*	.239	.111	−.010	−.058	.097	.006	.037	.100	.009	.053	.099
Harsh parenting	.044*	.302	.111	.005	.032	.096	.037*	.223	.100	−.023	−.130	.099
Maternal work hours (age 4)	−.002	.000	.004	−.012	−.002	.003				−.023	−.005	.005
Maternal work hours (age 6)							−.008	−.002	.005	−.032	−.006	.005
Maternal work hours (age 8)							.000	.000	.004	.022	.004	.003
Family income (age 4)	−.076*	−.259	.071	.001	.002	.063				−.043	−.120	.073
Family income (age 6)							.028	.082	.073	.001	.002	.068
Family income (age 8)							−.012	−.035	.062	−.026	−.069	.061
Biological father resident (age 4)	.023	.180	.153	−.042*	−.295	.132				.011	.069	.213
Biological father resident (age 6)							.032	.220	.200	.007	.045	.222
Biological father resident (age 8)							−.017	−.115	.183	−.019	−.115	.163
Stepfather resident (age 4)	.035*	.456	.223	.016	.180	.183				.016	.177	.193
Stepfather resident (age 6)							−.014	−.163	.194	.005	.054	.178
Stepfather resident (age 8)							.002	.020	.171	−.012	−.118	.145

Number of children (age 4)	.028	.087	.053	.004	.011	.047	−.024	−.066	.070	.014	.036	.075
Number of children (age 6)							.041	.105	.062	−.073*	−.178	.075
Number of children (age 8)										.038	.090	.059
Low self-regulation	.639*	4.962	.320	−.131*	−.889	.182	−.059*	−.401	.184	−.074*	−.472	.170
	$R^2 = .423$			$R^2 = .019$			$R^2 = .008$			$R^2 = .013$		

Model fit:

Likelihood ratio
$\chi^2 = 380.028$
df = 68. $p < .001$

CFI: .995
RMSEA: .028
90% CI RMSEA: .025–.031

*p < .05.

children, who had higher levels of EPB at age 4, exhibited a greater decline in EPB from 4 to 6 but it was not enough to bring them to the level of more regulated children.

Change in EPB from age 6 to 8. Neither family structure nor maternal employment was linked to change in EPB from 6 to 8. Less-regulated children's high level of EPB at age 4 remained high at age 6, even with a small reduction between 4 and 6 (Table 1), and they experienced a greater decline in EPB between ages 6 and 8 than those who were more regulated.

Change in EPB from age 8 to 10. Children who were less regulated at age 4 experienced continued but small declines in EPB between ages 8 and 10. Even after previous declines, the average level of EPB of less regulated children was higher at age 10 than that of children who were more regulated (a difference of 1.24; Table 1).

Externalizing problems by level of self-regulation

As shown above, self-regulation is an important predictor of children's EPB at age 4 and through age 10. When children were divided into high self-regulation (Table 4) and low self-regulation (Table 5) groups, the contribution of other environmental variables becomes clearer.

Overall level of EPB at age 4. The models for the overall level of EPB at age 4 (Intercept columns) are similar for children in the low and high regulation groups. One exception is that longer maternal work hours at age 4 were associated with having fewer EPB at age 4 only for less-regulated children. In the following sections, we summarize the association between father and stepfather residence with EPB, followed by maternal employment and EPB, by regulation group.

Father and stepfather residence

For the less-regulated children, living with a residential biological father at age 4 was associated with reduced EPB between ages 4 and 6 ($b = -.652$, effect size $= .17$) and living with a stepfather was also related to a reduction in EPB ($b = -.524$, effect size $= .14$) over that period. Family structure was not associated with EPB change for the more regulated group.

Living with a biological father at age 6 was associated with reduced EPB between 6 and 8 for more regulated children. Although this association was not significant for the group of children who were less regulated, later tests indicated that the coefficients did not differ across the groups. Therefore, we conclude that it is likely that living with the biological father at age 6 had the same association with EPB for less-regulated children. The association of stepfather residence at age 6 with EPB between ages 6 and 8 was not significant for either regulation group. Less-regulated children who lived with either a biological father or a step-parent at age 8 had a significantly lower risk of increased EPB between ages 8 and 10 compared with children who did not live with a stepparent or a biological father.

TABLE 4

Coefficients from the structural model of parent involvement, children who are more self-regulated (N = 3643)

| | A | | | B | | | C | | | D | | |
| | Intercept | | | Change age 4–6 | | | Change age 6–8 | | | Change age 8–10 | | |
Variable description	β	B	SE	β	b	SE	β	b	SE	β	b	SE
Mother's education	-.059*	-.077	.023	-.030	-.037	.024	.014	.017	.026	.025	.016	.025
Child female	-.019	-.120	.093	-.046*	-.281	.099	-.023	-.141	.101	.021	.174	.098
Child PPVT score	-.080*	-.014	.004	.028	.005	.004	.019	.003	.004	-.010	-.003	.004
Alcohol	.054*	.037	.011	.024	.016	.012	-.017	-.011	.013	.047*	.028	.012
Drug use	.068*	.432	.093	-.025	-.151	.100	.020	.118	.105	.009	.119	.101
Harsh parenting	.102*	.639	.092	-.012	-.074	.098	.005	.029	.102	-.020	-.095	.100
Maternal work hours (age 4)	**-.017**	**-.004**	.003	**-.014**	**-.003**	.004				**.049**	**.007**	.005
Maternal work hours (age 6)							**.024**	**.005**	.005	**.012**	**.001**	.005
Maternal work hours (age 8)							**-.031**	**-.006**	.004	**-.010**	**-.001**	.004
Family income (age 4)	-.100*	-.318	.062	-.031	-.095	.066				-.014	-.083	.081
Family income (age 6)							.026	.078	.078	-.032	-.070	.080
Family income (age 8)							.010	.032	.066	-.023	-.050	.078
Biological father resident (age 4)	-.014	-.096	.112	-.019	-.126	.119				.030	-.068	.180
Biological father resident (age 6)							.047	.313	.171	.004	.239	.203
Biological father resident (age 8)							-.068*	-.437	.153	-.008	-.120	.160
Stepfather resident (age 4)	.021	.227	.193	.035	**.362**	**.207**				.001	.197	.232
Stepfather resident (age 6)							-.010	-.106	.226	.026	.195	.181
Stepfather resident (age 8)							-.023	**-.238**	**.151**	-.020	-.182	.177

(continued)

TABLE 4 – Continued

Variable description	A Intercept			B Change age 4–6			C Change age 6–8			D Change age 8–10		
	β	B	SE	β	b	SE	β	b	SE	β	b	SE
Number of children (age 4)	−.015	−.041	.040	.023	.060	.043	.007	.019	.073	−.032	−.017	.079
Number of children (age 6)							.023	.058	.066	−.093*	−.169	.082
Number of children (age 8)										.069	.063	.063
	$R^2 = .062$			$R^2 = .009$			$R^2 = .005$			$R^2 = 0.012$		

Likelihood ratio
$\chi^2 = 84.891$
50 df, $p < .01$

Model fit:
CFI: .996
RMSEA: .017
90% CI RMSEA: .010–.023

Notes: Bolded coefficients differ across self-regulation groups.
*$p < .05$.

TABLE 5

Coefficients from the structural model of parent involvement, children who are less self-regulated ($N = 1324$)

	A			B			C			D		
	Intercept			Change age 4–6			Change age 6–8			Change age 8–10		
Variable description	β	b	SE	β	b	SE	β	b	SE	β	b	SE
Mother's education	−.077*	−.128	.028	−.024	−.036	.028	−.022	−.033	.029	−.019	−.019	.028
Child female	−.056*	−.435	.113	−.040*	−.281	.113	.009	.064	.116	.032	.207	.111
Child PPVT score	.010	.002	.004	.065*	.013	.004	−.031	−.006	.004	.047*	.009	.004
Alcohol	−.015	−.012	.013	−.002	−.001	.013	−.034	−.024	.014	.063*	.042	.013
Drug use	.058*	.450	.116	.030	.213	.116	.001	.010	.121	−.028	−.178	.115
Harsh parenting	.047*	.368	.113	−.014	−.096	.113	.075*	.526	.117	−.018	−.115	.112
Maternal work hours (age 4)	−.102*	**−.027**	.004	**.035***	**.008**	.004	**−.091***	**−.022**	.006	**.050**	**.011**	.006
Maternal work hours (age 6)							**.044***	**.010**	.005	**−.131***	**−.026**	.006
Maternal work hours (age 8)										**.052***	**.010**	.004
Family income (age 4)	−.095*	−.347	.072	.029	.096	.074	.021	.069	.086	.016	.048	.088
Family income (age 6)							−.012	−.038	.072	.069*	.206	.086
Family income (age 8)										−.055+	−.164	.084
Biological father resident (age 4)	.033	.260	.136	−.090*	−.652	.136	.037	.265	.194	−.022	−.143	.201
Biological father resident (age 6)							.016	.113	.172	.047	.302	.227
Biological father resident (age 8)										−.065*	−.421	.177
Stepfather resident (age 4)	.008	.133	.239	**−.035***	**−.524**	.239	−.004	−.066	.260	.007	.100	.262
Stepfather resident (age 6)							**.027**	**.318**	.172	.008	.089	.203
Stepfather resident (age 8)										−.045*	−.492	.197

(continued)

TABLE 5 – Continued

Variable description	A Intercept			B Change age 4–6			C Change age 6–8			D Change age 8–10		
	β	b	SE	β	b	SE	β	b	SE	β	b	SE
Number of children (age 4)	−.046*	−.142	.049	.029	.081	.049	−.018	−.050	.083	.009	.023	.089
Number of children (age 6)							−.025	−.069	.075	.031	.078	.092
Number of children (age 8)										.017	.042	.070
	$R^2 = .042$			$R^2 = .013$			$R^2 = .015$			$R^2 = .019$		

Model fit:

Likelihood ratio $\chi^2 = 84.891$ 50 df, $p < .01$

CFI: .996
RMSEA: .017
90% CI RMSEA: .010–.023

Notes: Bolded coefficients differ across self-regulation groups.

*$p < .05$.

Maternal employment. Maternal work hours played an important part in child EPB for the less-regulated group. Less-regulated 4-year-old children whose mothers worked more hours increased their EPB between ages 4 and 6 more than children of mothers who worked fewer hours, but the effect was small. Less-regulated children's EPB between ages 6 and 8 also increased slightly if the mother had a work hour increase when the child was age 6. However, this latter increase was offset by reduced behavioural problems between ages 6 and 8 if a work hour increase had occurred at age 4. Greater work hours at age 8 were associated with EPB growth between ages 8 and 10, but this was offset by a reduced EPB if the mother worked more when the child was age 6. Increased work hours were consistently associated with increased EPB in the subsequent 2 years, whereas after 2 years they reduced EPB.

Test for invariance across self-regulation groups. The overall fit for the multiple group analysis was excellent, with a CFI of .996 and an RMSEA of .017 with a 90% confidence interval of .010 to .023. The comparison of the model with all coefficients constrained to be equal across self-regulation groups to the unconstrained model indicated that the models were significantly different (χ^2 (50) = 84.891, $p < .01$). Not all variables differed across models. Our interest was whether the coefficients for father/stepfather residence and for maternal employment differed across self-regulation groups.

Although the individual coefficients for biological father residence were more likely to be statistically significant for children who were less regulated than more regulated, the coefficients were similar in size and direction ($\Delta\chi^2$ (7) = 6.689, *ns*), suggesting that the association between father residence and children's EPB is the same across self-regulation groups. For stepfathers, in contrast, tests for invariance confirmed that the association between stepfather residence and EPB varied across the self-regulation groups, particularly in the ages 4–6 and 6–8 transitions ($\Delta\chi^2$ (2) = 6.099, $p < .05$). Finally, the overall test for invariance confirmed that the association between maternal employment and child EPB differed across self-regulation groups ($\Delta\chi^2(7) = 16.094$, $p < .05$).

Differences in the associations between family structure, maternal employment and EPB across age groups, less regulated children

The latent difference model is justified if associations are likely to vary across age groups. Because the results do not differ by children's self-regulation for biological father residence, and there are no significant associations of either stepfather residence or maternal employment with EPB change for more regulated children, we summarize the results only for less-regulated children. The full table is provided as an Appendix available online. For biological father and stepfather residence, the 2-year associations with EPB (e.g., age 4 and ages

4–6 change compared with age 6 and 6–8 change) differed across ages. Only one set of lagged associations with EPB differed for biological fathers: between age 4 and ages 4–6 and age 4 and ages 6–8. There was no difference in lagged associations for stepfathers. For maternal employment, the 2-year associations did not differ, whereas all the lagged associations differed across ages.

DISCUSSION

Using a latent difference score model in a 4-wave nationally representative longitudinal study of US mothers, we explored how the timing of changes in family structure (father and stepfather residence) and maternal employment are associated with changes in children's EPB in early childhood from ages 4 to 10. We also examined whether these associations vary by children's level of self-regulation and age.

Controlling for family and child-level characteristics, we found that children's ability to self-regulate (assessed in this study as mothers' report of children's ability to inhibit responses and control their emotions) was most predictive of EPB at age 4. EPB began at a higher level and declined over time for less-regulated children, whereas levels were low and stable for more regulated children. Our hypothesis that family structure would be related to EPB at age 4 was partially supported. Living with a biological father was not associated with children's EPB at age 4, whereas living with a stepfather was initially associated with higher EPB. This finding supports research showing that a change in living arrangements—the introduction of a stepfather in the early years—is difficult for young children as they may be unable to deal with the emotional distress of not only having a new father figure but also not living with their biological fathers (Amato, 1993).

We found no support for our hypothesis that maternal employment at age 4 is associated with children's higher EPB at age 4. This finding is consistent with past studies that maternal employment is not harmful and might even be beneficial for children *after* the first year (Dunifon, Kalil, & Bajracharya, 2005; Han et al., 2001).

A central goal of this study was to examine how the association between changes in family structure (father and stepfather presence), maternal employment and EPB over ages 4–10 varied by children's level of self-regulation assessed at age 4. We found that living with a biological father at age 4 was protective for all children during the ages 4–6 transition to school, regardless of the level of self-regulation. But, supporting our third hypothesis, during important transitions such as entering school with its more rigid rules and structure, less-regulated children not only seem to benefit from living with their biological fathers but also benefit from living with a stepfather. Less-regulated children living with a stepfather at age 4 were reported to have fewer EPB during the transition to school (4–6) than those not living with a father. Similarly, living with a stepfather at age 8 was associated with a 11–12% standard deviation reduction in EPB from age 8 to 10, just prior to middle school, another sensitive period for children. These findings suggest that less-regulated children do better in households with either a biological father or stepfather. The benefits might be conferred directly and indirectly through positive effects on family functioning. It is worth reiterating, however, that initially (at age 4) the introduction of a stepfather into the household resulted in more EPB. The "initial shock to the system" of having a stepfather, particularly in the child's early years, may have created a temporary spike in EPB, but this is not sustained over time.

Our findings offer new information about the ways in which maternal employment might influence children's EPB over time. We found that maternal employment was linked to both *increases and decreases* in EPB, but only for less-regulated children, who might have difficulty coping with their mothers working longer hours. It had no association with EPB for more regulated children. We find that although greater employment hours at age 4 are associated with increased EPB during the transition to school—ages 4–6—they are also associated with decreased EPB at ages 6–8. This pattern of immediate increases in EPB after maternal employment change followed by lagged declines holds across the entire childhood period. This finding suggests that once children become used to increased maternal employment, and perhaps settle on a routine, the benefits of maternal employment (more money, less stress) might result in subsequent EPB decline.

Study limitations

The first limitation of this study was the lack of detailed information about family process during key transitions, father involvement and the father–child relationship prior to the child's age 10. The second limitation was the narrow measurement of self-regulation. Although unfortunate, it is important to reiterate that these questions were innovative 25 years ago when the study began. Offsetting these limitations is the large nationally representative sample, high data quality and advantage of having multiple waves of data following children and their behaviour for 6 years over the early and middle childhood period.

CONCLUSIONS

In conclusion, our findings show that fathers and stepfathers make an important difference in children's EPB over time, especially during transitions, a time of added stress for children. They support the view that fathers who live with their children have more opportunities to engage with them in ways that encourage social adaptation (Flanders et al., 2010). Although most children can cope with transitions, living with a biological father early (at age 4) is protective for children during the transition to school (at ages 4–6), and this does not differ by level of self-regulation. However, less-regulated children are more likely to have difficulties and hence the presence of a stepfather seems to be protective during these transitions. Maternal employment is associated with both increases and decreases in EPB; overall, it appears to be beneficial for children over time, although there may be an initial period of adjustment. This provides a more nuanced understanding of how more vulnerable children, those who have less ability to self-regulate, may react to changes in family structure and routines both immediately and over time.

FUNDING

Funding for this research was provided by the National Institute of Child Health and Human Development to Cornell University, through a subcontract to the University of Maryland [grant number P01-HD045610].

SUPPLEMENTARY MATERIAL

Supplementary Appendix is available via the 'Supplementary' tab on the article's online page.

REFERENCES

Achenbach, T., Dumenci, L., & Rescorla, L. (2003). Are American children's problems still getting worse? A 23-year comparison. *Journal of Abnormal Child Psychology*, *31*, 1–11.

Amato, P. (1993). Children's adjustment to divorce: Theories, hypotheses, empirical support. *Journal of Marriage and the Family*, *55*, 23–38.

Bachman, H. J., Coley, R. L., & Carrano, J. (2011). Maternal relationship instability influences on children's emotional and behavioral functioning in low-income families. *Journal of Abnormal Child Psychology*, *39*, 1149–1161.

Burgess, K. B., Marshall, P., Rubin, K. H., & Fox, N. A. (2003). Infant attachment and temperament as predictors of subsequent behavior problems and psychophysiological functioning. *Journal of Child Psychology and Psychiatry and Allied Disciplines*, *44*, 1–13.

Cabrera, N. J., Cook, G. A., McFadden, K., & Bradley, R. (2012). Father residence and father-child relationship quality: Peer relationships and externalizing behavior problems. *Family Science*, *1*, 1–11.

Cabrera, N., Shannon, J., & Tamis-LeMonda, C. (2007). Fathers' influence on their children's cognitive and emotional development: From toddlers to pre-K. *Applied Developmental Science*, *11*, 208–213.

Campbell, S. (1995). Behavior problems in preschool children: A review of recent research. *Journal of Child Psychology Psychiatry*, *36*, 113–149.

Campbell, S. B., Shaw, D. S., & Gilliom, M. (2000). Early externalizing behavior problems: Toddlers and preschoolers at risk for later maladjustment. *Development and Psychopathology*, *12*, 467–488.

Cavanagh, S., & Huston, A. (2008). The timing of family instability and children's social development. *Journal of Marriage and Family*, *70*, 1258–1269.

Center for Human Resource Research. (2004). *NLSY user guide, 1979–2004*. Columbus, OH: Center for Human Resource Research.

Coley, R. L., Lohman, B. J., Votruba-Drzal, E., Pittman, L. D., & Chase-Lansdale, P. L. (2007). Maternal functioning, time, and money: The world of work and welfare. *Children and Youth Services Review*, *29*, 721–741.

Collishaw, S., Gardner, F., Maughan, B., Scott, J., & Pickles, A. (2012). Do historical changes in parent-child relationships explain increases in youth conduct problems? *Journal of Abnormal Child Psychology, 40*, 119–132.

Cummings, E. M., El-Sheikh Kouros, C. D., & Buckhalt, J. (2009). Children and violence: The role of children's regulation in the marital aggression-child adjustment link. *Clinical Child and Family Psychology Review, 12*, 3–15.

Dunifon, R., Kalil, A., & Bajracharya, A. (2005). Maternal working conditions and child well-being in welfare-leaving families. *Developmental Psychology, 41*, 851–859.

Flanders, J., Simard, M., Paquette, D., Parent, S., Vitaro, F., Phil, R. O., & Seguin, J. R. (2010). Rough-and-tumble play and the development of physical aggression and emotion regulation: A five-year follow-up study. *Journal of Family Violence, 25*, 357–367. doi:10.1007/s10896-009-9297-5

Fomby, P., & Cherlin, A. (2007). Family instability and child well-being. *American Sociological Review, 72*, 181–204.

Grusec, J. (2011). Socialization processes in the family: Social and emotional development. *Annual Review of Psychology, 62*, 243–269.

Han, W. -J., Waldfogel, J., & Brooks-Gunn, J. (2001). The effects of early maternal employment on later cognitive and behavioral outcomes. *Journal of Marriage and Family, 63*, 336–354.

Haveman, R. H., & Wolfe, B. S. (1994). *Succeeding generations: On the effects of investments in children*. New York, NY: Russell Sage Foundation.

Hetherington, E., & Stanley-Hagan, M. (1995). Parenting in divorced and remarried families. In M. Bornstein (Ed.), *Handbook on parenting. Volume 3: Status and social conditions of parenting* (pp. 233–254). Mahwah, NJ: Lawrence Erlbaum.

Hofferth, S. L. (2006). Residential father family type and child well-being: Investment versus selection. *Demography, 43*, 53–77.

Johnson, R., Kalil, A., & Dunifon, R. (2012). Employment patterns of less-skilled workers: Links to children's behavior and academic progress. *Demography, 49*, 747–772.

Larsson, H., Viding, E., Rijsdijk, F., & Plomin, R. (2008). Relationships between parental negativity and childhood antisocial behavior over time: A bidirectional effects model in a longitudinal genetically informative design. *Journal of Abnormal Child Psychology, 36*, 633–645.

Leve, D. L., Kim, H., & Pears, K. C. (2005). Childhood temperament and family environment as predictors of internalizing and externalizing trajectories from ages 5 to 17. *Journal of Abnormal Child Psychology, 33*, 505–520.

Magnuson, K., & Berger, L. M. (2009). Family structure states and transitions: Associations with children's well-being during middle childhood. *Journal of Marriage and Family, 71*, 575–591.

McArdle, John J., & Hamagami, F. (2001). Latent difference score structural models for linear dynamic analyses with incomplete longitudinal data. In L. M. Collins & A. G. Sayer (Eds.), *New methods for the analysis of change, decade of behavior* (pp. 139–175). Washington, DC: American Psychological Association.

NICHD Early Childcare Research Network. (2004). Trajectories of physical aggression from toddlerhood to middle childhood. *Monographs of the Society for Research in Child Development, 69*, 1–146.

Osborne, C., & McLanahan, S. (2007). Partnership instability and child well-being. *Journal of Marriage and Family, 69*, 1065–1083.

Rothbart, M. K., Sheese, B. E., & Posner, M. I. (2007). Executive attention and effortful control: Linking temperament, brain networks, and genes. *Child Development Perspectives, 1*, 2–7.

Rubin, K., Burgess, K. B., Dwyer, K., & Hastings, P. (2003). Predicting preschoolers' externalizing behaviors from toddler temperament, conflict, and maternal negativity. *Developmental Psychology, 39*, 164–176.

Sayer, L. C., Bianchi, S. M., & Robinson, J. P. (2004). Are parents investing less in children? Trends in mothers' and fathers' time with children. *American Journal of Sociology, 110*, 1–43.

Tamis-LeMonda, C., Shannon, J., Cabrera, N., & Lamb, M. (2004). Fathers' and mothers' play with their 2- and 3-year-olds: Contributions to language and cognitive development. *Child Development, 75*, 1806–1820.

U.S. Census Bureau. (2012). *Statistical abstract of the United States, 2012*. Suitland, MD: U.S. Census Bureau.

Predicting adolescents' parent–child relationship quality from parental personality, marital conflict and adolescents' personality

Harald Werneck[1], Maximilian Oscar Eder[1], Takuya Yanagida[2], and Brigitte Rollett[1]

[1]Department of Applied Psychology: Health, Development, Enhancement and Intervention, Faculty of Psychology, University of Vienna, Vienna, Austria
[2]Research Center Linz, University of Applied Sciences Upper Austria, Linz, Austria

Longitudinal influences on the relationships between parents and their adolescent children in 175 Austrian families were analysed with data from three measurement points over a time span of 18 years. We investigated the influences of parental personality, marital conflict and adolescents' personality on the father–child and mother–child relationships separately. Inconsistent with previous theories and empirical findings, we found almost no associations between parental personality and parent–child relationships. Marital conflict was associated with only the father–child relationship. Children's personality showed the most consistent associations with the parent–child relationship. Our data support the theory of dynamic interactionism, which postulates an interdependency of personality factors and social relationships.

In his process model of parenting, Belsky (1984) postulated that there are three main sources that influence parental functioning: characteristics of parents and children (e.g., personality) on the one hand and contextual factors (e.g., the marital relationship) on the other. He hypothesized that parental personality should show the largest associations with aspects of the parent–child relationship (APCR) followed by contextual factors and children's personality. We used this model as a theoretical framework but decided to replace the expression *parenting* by *parent–child relationship* because the former " ... is unidirectional in nature and implies a causal primacy on the part of the parents" (Denissen, van Aken, & Dubas, 2009, p. 928).

Previous research has primarily focused on aspects of the mother–child relationship (AMCR); however, studies from the last two decades have suggested that there is also a notable connection between aspects of the father–child relationship (AFCR) and children's as well as fathers' personality (Asendorpf & van Aken, 2003; Metsapelto & Pulkkinen, 2003; Sturaro, Denissen, van Aken, & Asendorpf, 2008).

Earlier literature has extensively focused on the interplay between characteristics of fathers, mothers, children and APCR with some studies taking into account discrete personality characteristics (e.g., self-esteem), whereas a growing body of literature has used the five factor theory (FFT) as a measurement framework (Asendorpf & Wilpers, 1998; Denissen et al., 2009; O'Connor & Dvorak, 2001; Prinzie et al., 2004; Sturaro et al., 2008). We adopted this approach and will discuss the interplay of parental personality, the marital relationship and children's personality with APCR.

Parental personality and APCR

A review by Belsky and Barends (2002) investigated associations between the Big Five factors and APCR. In summary, conscientiousness was found to be positively related to supportive parenting, but empirical evidence was limited, and other authors failed to report a significant association (Denissen et al., 2009). Also, in summary, APCR were positively associated with parental depressive mood and negatively related to parental sensitivity and nurturance, findings that were supported by Metsapelto and Pulkkinen (2003). Similarly, extraversion was positively associated with supportive parenting and warmth, which was also supported by other studies (Denissen et al., 2009; Metsapelto & Pulkkinen, 2003). Additionally, agreeableness was positively associated with parental responsiveness in summary, although other authors have reported null-findings (e.g., Denissen et al., 2009). Finally, openness was negatively associated with parental restrictiveness and restrictive parental control (Denissen et al., 2009; Metsapelto & Pulkkinen, 2003).

While one study found that the associations between APCR and parental personality differ for fathers and mothers (Belsky, Crnic, & Woodworth, 1995), others have failed to report clear differences (Denissen et al., 2009; Metsapelto & Pulkkinen, 2003). Thus, irrespective of parental gender, there seems to be agreement that APCR are associated with the dimensions of the FFT, although compelling evidence exists to a greater extent for some dimensions (neuroticism, extraversion, openness) than for others (conscientiousness, agreeableness). We therefore expected a significant positive association of paternal/maternal emotional stability, extraversion and openness, but no associations of agreeableness and conscientiousness with positive AFCR/AMCR.

The marital relationship and APCR

Contextual factors, marital relationship quality in particular, should also be included in the process model of parenting when investigating APCR. Marital quality (i.e., marital communication, tenderness and conflict behaviour) influences parents' relationship satisfaction and has a direct impact on APCR (Riggio, 2004; Shek, 2000). A meta-analytic review indicated positive significant relations between marital quality and APCR and other authors suggested that parental behaviours have a long-lasting influence of up to 12 years on APCR (Booth & Amato, 1994; Erel & Burman, 1995). Although some studies have investigated different aspects of the marital relationship, others have emphasized marital conflict as an important variable (Riggio, 2004). Furthermore, marital quality has been shown to be more strongly associated with AFCR than with AMCR because the parental role is less central and thus more susceptible to influence for fathers than for mothers (Belsky, Youngblade, Rovine, & Volling, 1991; Booth & Amato, 1994).

Two main hypotheses are discussed in the literature to explain the relation between APCR and marital quality. The compensatory framework hypothesis implies that positive parental marital quality has a negative effect on APCR (Erel & Burman, 1995). Hence, a lack of positive attributes in the parental relationship would be balanced by positive patterns in APCR. However, only a few studies have empirically supported this hypothesis (e.g., Belsky et al., 1991). By contrast, the spill-over perspective implies that positive attributes of marital relations foster APCR. This perspective has been supported by previous findings (Booth & Amato, 1994; Erel & Burman, 1995; Riggio, 2004). Thus, taking Belsky's model into account (Belsky, 1984), we expected that marital conflict would be more strongly associated with AFCR than with AMCR, even after a considerable amount of time and after controlling for the effects of paternal/maternal personality.

Child personality and APCR

Adolescents' conscientiousness has been reported to predict contact frequency with parents, more parental support and the use of inductive reasoning by parents (Asendorpf & Wilpers, 1998; Asendorpf & van Aken, 2003; O'Connor & Dvorak, 2001). While some studies have found negative associations of children's neuroticism with APCR (e.g., parental support; O'Connor & Dvorak, 2001; Sturaro et al., 2008), most authors have reported null findings between those variables (e.g., Denissen et al., 2009). Children's extraversion has been positively related to APCR, although findings are limited (e.g., Zhong-Hui, Hui-Lan, & Jian-Xin, 2006). Agreeableness has shown negative associations with parental harshness, coerciveness and negative behaviour, whereas it has been positively associated with parental warmth (O'Connor & Dvorak, 2001; Prinzie et al., 2004; Zhong-Hui et al., 2006). Finally, to our knowledge, there is no clear empirical evidence for relations between APCR and openness.

Few of the studies reported earlier explicitly investigated whether these associations differ by parental gender. When indicators of these associations were reported, they differed only slightly for AFCR and AMCR (Asendorpf & van Aken, 2003; Prinzie et al., 2004; Sturaro et al., 2008), although some authors have implied that AFCR shows a larger association with children's personality than AMCR (Asendorpf & van Aken, 2003; Sturaro et al., 2008).

As with parental personality factors, clear evidence is available for some factors (conscientiousness, agreeableness) more than for others (neuroticism, extraversion, openness). Taking into account the hypothesized order of importance of the sources influencing APCR (Belsky, 1984), we expected significant positive associations of children's agreeableness and conscientiousness, but no associations of emotional stability, extraversion and openness, with positive AFCR/AMCR, even after effects of paternal/maternal personality and marital relationship were controlled for. Due to a dearth of studies reporting differences for fathers and mothers, we had no explicit expectation of how the results might differ by parental gender.

Although previous findings have reported considerable associations between children's personality and APCR, it remains unclear whether one of the two variables causally precedes the other or whether they show an interdependent relation. Asendorpf and Wilpers (1998) found impacts of children's personality on APCR, but could not find impacts of APCR on personality, findings that were supported by other studies (Asendorpf & van Aken, 2003; Neyer & Asendorpf, 2001). Conversely, other findings have implied that there are no direct effects of children's personality on APCR, but that there seems to be a reverse effect (Sturaro et al., 2008). The findings of personality effects on relationships in the absence of reverse effects would strengthen the perspective that is imposed by the FFT (McCrae et al., 2000). The FFT implies that basic personality tendencies such as the Big Five personality traits are endogenous and thus cannot be environmentally influenced. Accordingly, one would expect that personality factors would have an influence on APCR but not vice versa. Conversely, approaches based on the theory of interactionism postulate that environmental factors (e.g., relationships) interact with personality and are able to alter it in different ways (Reynolds et al., 2010). These theories imply an interaction between APCR and personality and thus an influence from both groups of variables. As there is currently a broader empirical fundament for the FFT (McCrae et al., 2000), we expected significant influences from children's conscientiousness and agreeableness, but not from extraversion, openness and neuroticism on APCR but not vice versa.

This study focussed on the main influences on APCR postulated by Belsky (1984). We aimed to investigate the associations of parental personality, marital relationships and children's personality with AFCR/AMCR for adolescents. This time period represents an interesting stage of emerging independence from the family environment. Thus, it seems important to increase knowledge about APCR as they might serve as important sources of support during this stage of development (e.g., O'Connor & Dvorak, 2001).

METHOD

Participants

Our analyses and results are based on the longitudinal project "Family Development in the Course of Life" (Rollett, Werneck, & Hanfstingl, 2009). Data were initially collected from 175 parental couples and 175 children (88 male) at seven time points. For the current analyses, Times 2, 6 and 7 were included, when children were 3 months, 15 years and 18 years of age. The children's ages ranged from 17 to 19 years ($M = 17.74$, SD $= 0.48$) at Time 7. Participants were recruited in the larger Vienna area via maternity institutions. Some participants were not able to attend all data collection sessions. At Time 7, there were still 143 mothers (81.7%), 119 fathers (68.0%) and 142 children (81.1%) participating; thus, the drop-out quota over a period of about 18 years can be considered comparatively low.

Missing data

In total, 96 of 178 family records (46.3%) were incomplete. The percentage of missing values across the 25 variables varied between 6.2% and 34.3%. We used multiple imputation (Rubin, 1987) to deal with the missing data. Incomplete variables were imputed under fully conditional specification (Van Buuren, Brand, Groothuis-Oudshoorn, & Rubin, 2006) resulting in 30 multiple imputed data-sets. The imputation model included the 25 variables that appeared in one or more of the subsequent regression analyses. Calculations were done in R (R Development Core Team, 2013) using the mice package (Van Buuren & Groothuis-Oudshoorn, 2011). Statistical analyses were computed on each imputed data-set separately and subsequently pooled using Rubin's rules (1987) to combine the parameter estimates and standard errors into a single set of results. Methodologists currently regard multiple imputation as a state-of-the-art technique because it improves accuracy and statistical power relative to other missing data handling methods (Schafer & Graham, 2002).

Measures

Aspects of parent–child relationship. The inventory of parent and peer attachment (IPPA; Armsden & Greenberg, 1987; translated and adapted for preadolescents, Werneck & Rollett, 2007) was used to measure APCR. The three original scales are trust (8 items; α t6 [AMCR/AFCR] = .77/.88, α t7 [AMCR/AFCR] = .88/.87, e.g., "I trust my mother/father"), communication (8 items; α t6 [AMCR/AFCR] = .85/.87, α t7 [AMCR/AFCR] = .86/.87, e.g., "I tell my mother/father about my problems and troubles") and alienation (5 items; α t6 [AMCR/AFCR] = .70/.68, α t7 [AMCR/AFCR] = .72/.75, e.g., "I get upset a lot more than my mother/father knows"). Principal components analysis with varimax rotation resulted in an additional fourth factor called negative emotional ties (5 items; α t6 [AMCR/AFCR] = .69/.70, α t7 [AMCR/AFCR] = .69/.68, e.g., "I wish I had different parents"). Values on each scale range from 1 to 5. We used children's reports from t6 and t7 in these analyses.

Personality. The German version of the NEO Five Factor Inventory (NEO-FFI; Borkenau & Ostendorf, 1993) was used to assess aspects of children's and parents' personality including the scales neuroticism (6 items; α [child] t6 = .78, α t7 [child/mother/father] = .78/.85/.77), extraversion (6 items; α t6 [child] = .71, α t7 [child/mother/father] = .71/.72/.74), openness (6 items; α t6 [child] = .76, α t7 [child/mother/father] = .76/.71/.76), agreeableness (6 items; α t6 [child] = .73, α t7 [child/mother/father] = .78/.73/.70) and conscientiousness (6 items; α t6 [child] = .83, α t7 [child/mother/father] = .73/.68/.73). Values range from 1 to 5 on each scale. We used reports from children (t6 and t7) and from both parents (t7).

Marital quality. The partnership questionnaire (PFB; Hahlweg, 1979) was used to measure marital quality. It originally consisted of three scales. For this article, we used only the conflict behaviour scale (10 items; α t2 [mother/father] = .83/.89, e.g., "When we quarrel, he/she showers me with insults"). Values on each scale range from 1 to 4. We used mother's and father's assessments of their partner's conflict behaviour at Time 2.

Procedure

Data were collected via home visits. The families were visited by trained interviewers who conducted various tests and handed over the relevant documents. Every mother, father and child was asked to complete the documents separately.

Analytic strategy

To address our hypotheses on the relations between parental and children's personality, marital conflict and APCR, we computed a series of multivariate hierarchical regression analyses using Mplus 7 (Muthén & Muthén, 2012).

We used the NEO-FFI scales at Time 7 for all subjects and the partner conflict scale for parents from the PFB at Time 2 as predictors and the IPPA scales for AFCR/AMCR at Time 7 as the dependent variables. The regression models were computed for mothers and fathers separately. Predictors were entered hierarchically and were forced into the regression equation at each step. For the process model of parenting, the NEO-FFI scales for parents were entered into the equation in the first step, followed by partner conflict in the second step, and the NEO-FFI scales for children in the third step.

To address our hypothesis on the nature of the relation between children's personality and APCR, we analysed the associations of the two variables across two time points using cross-lagged panel models as depicted in Figure 1. If one considers the correlational pattern in Figure 1, where APCR and children's personality (P) are shown for two time points of measurement ($APCR_{1,2}$, $P_{1,2}$), it is possible to analyse the association of $APCR_1$ with P_2 while controlling for their correlation at two time points as well as for their stability over time. We were limited to conducting this relation for the interplay of APCR and children's personality only because no parental personality data were present prior to Time 7. To conduct the path analysis, we used AMOS 5. We calculated 40 models each using a different combination of the variables (five different variables for children's personality and four for AFCR/AMCR) for fathers and mothers separately. As stated by Neyer and Asendorpf (2001), this type of modelling is very useful for analysing temporal effects between two variables because it is able to control for previous effects of the two variables and their temporal stability.

RESULTS

Results of the multivariate multiple regression models for APCR are reported in Tables 1 and 2. We expected to find significant relations between parental personality and APCR. These were generally not supported by our data.

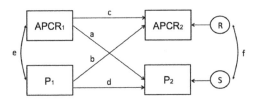

Figure 1. Conceptual cross-lagged panel model linking the parent–child relationship ($APCR_{1,2}$) and children's personality ($P_{1,2}$) over two time points while controlling for the variables' long-term stability, their initial correlation, and the correlated change between the parent–child relationship and children's personality at Time 2. Path coefficients are represented by the letters a–d, and the initial correlation and the correlation between the residuals of the parent–child relationship and children's personality (R, S) are represented by e and f.

TABLE 1

Results of the multivariate hierarchical regression analysis predicting the four IPPA scales for fathers at Time 7 using father's personality at Time 7, partner conflict at Time 2 and child's personality at Time 7 as predictors

	Trust			Communication			Negative emotional ties			Alienation		
	β	SE	R²	β	SE	R²	β	SE	R²	β	SE	R²
Step 1												
Father's personality												
Neuroticism (t7)	.139	.118		.065	.116		.072	.126		.097	.109	
Extraversion (t7)	.036	.136		.123	.128		.092	.133		.028	.123	
Openness (t7)	.058	.105		.038	.097		−.040	.100		.000	.098	
Agreeableness (t7)	.193*	.096		.137	.091		−.167	.097		−.144	.092	
Conscientiousness (t7)	−.004	.102	.072	.057	.112	.063	−.031	.097	.049	−.117	.100	.064
Step 2												
Father's personality												
Neuroticism (t7)	.148	.109		.072	.110		.062	.122		.090	.109	
Extraversion (t7)	.026	.125		.116	.120		.099	.123		.034	.120	
Openness (t7)	.076	.098		.052	.093		−.058	.095		−.011	.097	
Agreeableness (t7)	.100	.095		.066	.093		−.082	.095		−.088	.094	
Conscientiousness (t7)	.007	.096		.065	.108		−.040	.088		−.124	.101	
Partner conflict (t2)	−.353**	.088	.187**	−.270**	.093	.130*	.318**	.082	.142**	.211*	.089	.107*
Step 3												
Father's personality												
Neuroticism (t7)	.126	.102		−.002	.101		.080	.110		.135	.102	
Extraversion (t7)	−.006	.118		.071	.112		.105	.112		.064	.114	
Openness (t7)	.082	.094		.023	.089		−.039	.083		.019	.096	
Agreeableness (t7)	.101	.093		.048	.085		−.091	.090		−.080	.093	

	β	SE	β	SE	β	SE	β	SE
Conscientiousness (t7)	−.085	.093	−.035	.104	.062	.084	−.035	.101
Partner conflict (t2)	−.354**	.086	−.258**	.089	.269**	.074	.179*	.087
Child's personality								
Neuroticism (t7)	−.143	.082	−.107	.080	.403**	.082	.218*	.090
Extraversion (t7)	.155	.086	.181*	.090	−.033	.087	−.152	.091
Openness (t7)	.151*	.073	.307**	.071	−.105	.074	−.181*	.084
Agreeableness (t7)	.074	.086	−.007	.092	.087	.083	.079	.088
Conscientiousness (t7)	.147*	.075	.111	.079	−.083	.079	−.043	.084
R^2	.302**		.282**		.330**		.228**	

Notes: The analyses were computed separately for each IPPA scale and subdivided in a stepwise manner. β, standardized regression coefficient; SE, standard error; R^2, coefficient of determination.
*$p < .05$ and **$p < .01$.

TABLE 2

Results of the multivariate hierarchical regression analysis predicting the four IPPA scales for mothers at Time 7, using father's personality at Time 7, partner conflict at Time 2 and child's personality at Time 7 as predictors

	Trust			Communication			Negative emotional ties			Alienation		
	β	SE	R^2	β	SE	R^2	β	SE	R^2	β	SE	R^2
Step 1												
Mother's personality												
Neuroticism (t7)	.072	.102		.079	.102		.168	.114		−.007	.101	
Extraversion (t7)	.200*	.100		.240*	.104		−.141	.104		−.267*	.114	
Openness (t7)	−.003	.079		.129	.083		−.015	.074		−.054	.085	
Agreeableness (t7)	.094	.097		−.005	.085		−.028	.082		.036	.081	
Conscientiousness (t7)	−.031	.087	.050	.010	.081	.068	.057	.085	.083	−.009	.075	.077
Step 2												
Mother's personality												
Neuroticism (t7)	.071	.102		.080	.102		.167	.114		−.006	.100	
Extraversion (t7)	.194	.101		.242*	.106		−.141	.105		−.261*	.116	
Openness (t7)	.000	.077		.129	.082		.014	.073		−.057	.085	
Agreeableness (t7)	.078	.100		−.001	.088		−.024	.089		.052	.085	
Conscientiousness (t7)	−.026	.087		.010	.081		.055	.085		−.014	.076	
Partner conflict (t2)	−.051	.101	.056	.010	.096	.071	.013	.104	.086	.052	.100	.082
Step 3												
Mother's personality												
Neuroticism (t7)	.084	.093		.068	.096		.107	.101		−.024	.088	
Extraversion (t7)	.130	.092		.193*	.097		−.113	.093		−.225*	.101	
Openness (t7)	.022	.075		.124	.073		−.003	.073		−.059	.081	
Agreeableness (t7)	.055	.090		−.018	.080		−.001	.078		.065	.080	

	β	SE	β	SE	β	SE	β	SE
Conscientiousness (t7)	−.022	.080	−.003	.076	.040	.076	−.028	.072
Partner conflict (t2)	−.086	.092	−.003	.087	.048	.089	−.066	.091
Child's personality								
Neuroticism (t7)	−.250**	.082	−.143	.087	.392**	.077	.220**	.084
Extraversion (t7)	.089	.088	.057	.091	.029	.090	−.031	.089
Openness (t7)	.121	.082	.209**	.079	−.104	.086	−.168*	.081
Agreeableness (t7)	.099	.081	.147	.081	−.150	.078	−.201**	.078
Conscientiousness (t7)	.158*	.079	.180*	.082	−.078	.075	−.054	.081
	.216**		.229**		.289**		.232**	

Notes: The analyses were computed separately for each IPPA scale and subdivided in a stepwise manner. β, standardized regression coefficient; SE, standard error; R^2, coefficient of determination.
*p < .05 and **p < .01.

For AMCR, maternal extraversion showed significant associations, which we expected from the literature, although neuroticism and openness showed no such relations. In contrast to mother's personality, paternal personality showed no significant associations when other theoretically relevant variables were added.

Furthermore, we expected to find larger associations between parental conflict behaviour and AFCR as compared to AMCR. These were supported by our data. Paternal conflict behaviour as experienced by the mother at Time 2 showed a significant association with every facet of AFCR. No such relations were found for AMCR.

Our expectations that children's agreeableness and conscientiousness but not emotional stability, extraversion and openness would be positively associated with APCR were substantiated only partially. Slightly different patterns of associations emerged for mothers and fathers.

There were scattered associations between all child personality factors (except one) and AFCR. Conscientiousness showed a small but significant association with trust, whereas agreeableness failed to achieve significant associations with AFCR. Unexpectedly, the most consistent associations were found for children's openness, which was related to all AFCR variables except negative emotional ties. Children's neuroticism was positively related to negative emotional ties and alienation, and extraversion was positively related to communication.

Consistent with our expectations, children's agreeableness and conscientiousness showed significant associations with AMCR. Contrary to our hypothesis, openness and neuroticism also showed significant associations. In fact, neuroticism showed the largest and most consistent associations with AMCR.

The β's and standard errors for the cross-lagged panel models are reported in Tables 3 and 4. The β's indicate the cross-sectional path ("a"/"b" in Figure 1) from the hypothesized influential variable on the outcome variable while controlling for the stability of each variable over time and the correlation of the two variables at Times 6 and 7. The model fit was perfect for all models because they were completely saturated.

Table 3 displays the effects of children's personality at Time 6 on APCR at Time 7. Contrary to our expectation that there would be significant paths leading from children's personality (conscientiousness and agreeableness) to APCR, we found none for fathers. A different pattern resulted for mothers. In contrast to our expectations, agreeableness and conscientiousness showed no significant relations with AMCR reported by children. On the contrary, there were positive associations between children's extraversion and perceived trust and communication with the mother and a negative association with negative emotional ties. In addition, there were positive paths from children's openness to trust and communication and a negative path to alienation. To reduce the probability of Type I errors, we applied a Bonferroni correction for the 40 statistical tests. The critical p value for each path coefficient was thus changed to

TABLE 3
Cross-lagged path coefficients (path b) indicating the effect of aspects of children's personality (P_1) at Time 6 on AFCR/AMCR ($APCR_2$) at Time 7

	Trust		Negative emotional ties		Communication		Alienation	
	β	SE	β	SE	β	SE	β	SE
Child's personality	*Father–child relationship*							
Neuroticism	.02	.074	.01	.073	−.03	.093	.09	.099
Extraversion	.11	.092	−.04	.085	.09	.116	−.06	.118
Openness	.03	.073	-.06	.068	.07	.093	-.06	.093
Agreeableness	−.07	.105	.01	.101	−.08	.132	.00	.136
Conscientiousness	−.07	.070	.11	.067	−.06	.089	.06	.089
Child's personality	*Mother–child relationship*							
Neuroticism	.02	.070	−.01	.072	.06	.084	.00	.089
Extraversion	.26**	.081	−.22**	.080	.20*	.102	−.13	.104
Openness	.18*	.065	−.08	.066	.16*	.081	−.19*	.082
Agreeableness	−.04	.095	−.06	.097	−.04	.118	.00	.121
Conscientiousness	−.05	.065	.07	.065	−.01	.080	.01	.079

Notes: The results are presented separately for father–child and mother–child relationships. β, path coefficient; SE, standard error.
*$p < .05$ and **$p < .01$.

TABLE 4
Cross-lagged path coefficients (path a) indicating the effect of AFCR/AMCR ($APCR_1$) at Time 6 on aspects of children's personality (P_2) at Time 7

	Child's personality									
	Neuroticism		Extraversion		Openness		Agreeableness		Con- scientiousness	
	β	SE	β	SE	β	SE	β	SE	β	SE
Father–child relationship										
Trust	−.17*	.084	.04	.064	−.15	.091	.14	.073	−.05	.079
Negative emotional ties	.22**	.087	−.01	.063	.06	.092	−.11	.075	.10	.081
Communication	−.22**	.069	.08	.053	−.09	.077	.20*	.060	−.11	.066
Alienation	.17*	.079	−.07	.057	.05	.083	−.08	.067	.03	.071
Mother–child relationship										
Trust	−.24**	.120	.02	.092	−.10	.130	.11	.103	−.10	.114
Negative emotional ties	.24**	.092	−.02	.066	.01	.098	−.05	.079	.06	.085
Communication	−.19*	.077	.07	.058	−.03	.085	.18*	.066	−.12	.072
Alienation	.14	.081	−.04	.058	.03	.084	−.03	.068	.07	.070

Notes: The results are presented separately for father–child and mother–child relationships. β, path coefficient; SE, standard error.
*$p < .05$ and **$p < .01$.

$p = .00125$. The path from extraversion to trust survived the application of the strict criterion and remained significant.

Table 4 displays the effects of APCR at Time 6 on children's personality at Time 7. We expected to find no significant paths from APCR to children's personality. Contrary to this expectation, we found significant paths from APCR to neuroticism and agreeableness, although the pattern differed slightly for mothers and fathers. As can be seen in Table 4, all facets of AFCR showed a uniform effect on children's neuroticism. We found a similar pattern for mothers, although the path from alienation to neuroticism failed to reach significance ($p = .087$). Communication with fathers and mothers showed a similar path to children's agreeableness. Again, a Bonferroni correction was applied. Unfortunately, none of the formerly significant paths survived the application of this strict criterion.

DISCUSSION

This paper aimed to investigate different influences on APCR as assumed by Belsky's process model of parenting (Belsky, 1984). We conducted several regression analyses for AFCR and AMCR separately to test the assumptions that parental and children's personality and marital conflict are associated with APCR.

Contrary to our expectations, we found no significant associations between paternal personality and AFCR. There were also only a few significant associations between maternal personality and AMCR. Thus, in line with previous findings, the predominantly nonsignificant relations were similar for both parents (Denissen et al., 2009; Metsapelto & Pulkkinen, 2003).

This absence of significant relations is interesting because Belsky postulated that parental personality factors should in theory be the most important variables that influence APCR. Furthermore, these results are not consistent with previous empirical findings that have reported significant associations (Denissen et al., 2009; Metsapelto & Pulkkinen, 2003). On the one hand, this could be due to the fact that previous studies used the same sources of information for measuring APCR and parental personality, whereas the current study utilized two different sources. On the other hand, it is possible that children in this age group generally spend less time with their parents due to increasing contacts with peers. Less contact could possibly lower the associations between parental personality factors and APCR. Consistent with this notion, it is possible that contact with both parents is lowered to a similar degree resulting in comparable findings.

In line with our expectations, we found stronger associations of marital conflict with AFCR than with AMCR. In contrast to AFCR, AMCR were not associated with marital conflict as expressed 18 years earlier. We assume that marital conflict behaviour remains relatively stable over the years, thus leading to continuing parental conflict behaviour. The spill-over perspective implies that positive attributes of marital relations foster APCR. As high values in marital conflict were associated with low APCR quality, this perspective was supported by our results and by previous findings (e.g., Booth & Amato, 1994; Erel & Burman, 1995). Evidence has suggested that this effect is more present for fathers (e.g., Booth & Amato, 1994; Shek, 2000), explainable, for example, by the gate-keeping effects of the mothers. When fathers express conflict behaviour, mothers might regulate their contact with the child, which may worsen APCR. This assumption was supported by our data because there was no association between maternal conflict behaviour as perceived by the father and AMCR.

Consistent with our expectations, there were significant associations of children's agreeableness and conscientiousness with APCR. Unexpectedly, children's neuroticism and openness also showed significant associations with APCR, and extraversion showed a significant relation to communication with fathers. Interestingly, this pattern differed only marginally for fathers and mothers. This finding might reflect a shift of parental roles to become more similar. The assimilation of paternal and maternal involvement in parenting could provide comparable possibilities of children's characteristics to shape APCR.

In summary, the hypothesized order of importance of the variables included in the process model of parenting was not reflected by our data-set. Parental personality factors showed only a few associations with APCR, whereas marital conflict was associated with AFCR only. Interestingly, the theoretically least important source of influence showed the most consistent associations with APCR.

Our findings on the nature of the associations of children's personality with APCR contradicted our expectations. Contrary to our hypothesis, we found significant paths from all APCR factors to children's personality. Interestingly, these associations were observed predominantly for neuroticism. This is consistent with findings by Sturaro et al. (2008), who found a positive influence of conflict with fathers and mothers on children's neuroticism. We found a surprisingly similar pattern for fathers and mothers, which is also consistent with Sturaro et al.'s (2008) results. Children experiencing little parental support may become more prone to psychological distress and feelings of insecurity. In addition, communication with fathers and mothers showed a positive path to agreeableness. Children who describe opportunities to communicate with their parents in a forthright manner might tend to be more cooperative with other people. Overall, children's relationships with their mothers and their fathers showed intriguingly similar associations with children's personality.

For AMCR but not for AFCR, reversed associations were also found. Children's extraversion and openness at the age of 15 showed significant paths to AMCR 3 years later. It is possible that mothers spend more time with their children during this developmental phase than fathers, making their relationship more susceptible to children's characteristics.

Nevertheless, there are discrepancies between the results of the two analytical approaches, and these discrepancies are difficult to interpret. For instance, neuroticism did not show significant paths to AMCR in the cross-lagged panel models, but it was associated with AMCR in the regression models. This of course could be due to the fact that the significant results in the regression analyses actually originate from an effect of AMCR on neuroticism. However, there are also deviations between the analytical approaches for all remaining personality facets of children. Because the regression models covered variables only from Time 7, it is possible that the deviations in results suggest that the observed associations are variable over the course of development.

Altogether, these results do not support the assumptions of the FFT, which would imply significant paths from personality to APCR but not vice versa (McCrae et al., 2000). On the contrary, we found more paths leading from APCR to personality, but some reverse effects were found. This pattern of results supports the theory of dynamic interactionism, which postulates that personality and environment are interdependent factors that influence each other.

Limitations

There are some restrictions on the interpretability of our results due to the informants we used for the different measures. Most associations between personality factors and APCR were found for children, who also rated APCR. Of course, these effects could possibly be a manifestation of shared method variance, which would limit our criticism of Belsky's theory. Future research will need to include measures of APCR that are rated by both sides of the relationship. There also seem to be relevant factors that determine APCR other than those used in the current study or as proposed by Belsky's model. There is still some unexplained variance left in APCR. Children's gender as well as other influential contextual variables could be included in future analyses.

REFERENCES

Armsden, G., & Greenberg, M. T. (1987). The inventory of parent peer attachment: Individual differences and their relation to psychological well-being in adolescence. *Journal of Youth and Adolescence, 16*, 427–454.

Asendorpf, J. B., & van Aken, M. A. G. (2003). Personality–relationship transaction in adolescence: Core versus surface personality characteristics. *Journal of Personality, 71*, 629–666.

Asendorpf, J. B., & Wilpers, S. (1998). Personality effects on social relationships. *Journal of Personality and Social Psychology, 74*, 1531–1544.

Belsky, J. (1984). The determinants of parenting: A process model. *Child Development, 55*, 83–96.

Belsky, J., & Barends, N. (2002). Personality and parenting. In M. H. Bornstein (Ed.), *Handbook of parenting* (pp. 415–438). Mahwah, NJ: Erlbaum.

Belsky, J., Crnic, K., & Woodworth, S. (1995). Personality and parenting: Exploring the mediating role of transient mood and daily hassles. *Journal of Personality, 63*, 905–929.

Belsky, J., Youngblade, L., Rovine, M., & Volling, B. (1991). Patterns of marital change and parent–child interaction. *Journal of Marriage and the Family, 53*, 487–498.

Booth, A., & Amato, P. R. (1994). Parental marital quality, parental divorce, and relations with parents. *Journal of Marriage and Family, 56*, 21–34.

Borkenau, P., & Ostendorf, F. (1993). *NEO-Fünf-Faktoren-Inventar (NEO-FFI) nach Costa und McCrae (Handanweisung).* Göttingen: Hogrefe.

Denissen, J. J. A., van Aken, M. A. G., & Dubas, J. S. (2009). It takes two to tango: How parents' and adolescents' personalities link to the quality of their mutual relationship. *Developmental Psychology, 45*, 928–941.

Erel, O., & Burman, B. (1995). Interrelatedness of marital relations and parent–child relations: A meta-analytic review. *Psychological Bulletin, 118*, 108–132.

Hahlweg, K. (1979). Konstruktion und Validierung des Partnerschaftsfragebogens (PFB). *Zeitschrift für Klinische Psychologie, 8*, 17–40.

McCrae, R. R., Costa, P. T., Ostendorf, F., Angleitner, A., Hrebíčková, M., Avia, M. D., …, Smith, P. B. (2000). Nature over nurture: Temperament, personality, and life span development. *Journal of Personality and Social Psychology, 78*, 173–186.

Metsapelto, R. L., & Pulkkinen, L. (2003). Personality traits and parenting: Neuroticism, extraversion, and openness to experience as discriminative factors. *European Journal of Personality, 17*, 59–78.

Muthén, L. K., & Muthén, B. O. (2012). *Mplus user's guide* (7th ed.). Los Angeles, CA: Muthén & Muthén.

Neyer, F. J., & Asendorpf, J. B. (2001). Personality–relationship transaction in young adulthood. *Journal of Personality and Social Psychology, 81*, 1190–1204.

O'Connor, B. P., & Dvorak, T. (2001). Conditionals associations between parental behavior and adolescents problems: A search for personality–environment interactions. *Journal of Research in Personality, 35*, 1–26.

Prinzie, P., Onghena, P., Hellickx, W., Grietens, H., Ghesquiere, P., & Colpin, H. (2004). Parent and child personality characteristics as predictors of negative discipline and externalizing problem behaviour in children. *European Journal of Personality, 18*, 73–102.

R Development Core Team. (2013). *R: A language and environment for statistical computing.* Vienna: R Foundation for Statistical Computing.

Reynolds, K. J., Turner, J. C., Branscombe, N. R., Mavor, K. I., Bizumic, B., & Subasic, E. (2010). Interactionism in personality and social psychology: An integrated approach to understanding the mind and behaviour. *European Journal of Personality, 24*, 458–482.

Riggio, H. R. (2004). Parental marital conflict and divorce, parent–child relationships, social support, and relationship anxiety in young adulthood. *Personal Relationships, 11*, 99–114.

Rollett, B., Werneck, H., & Hanfstingl, B. (2009). Elterliche Partnerschaftsqualität und die Entwicklung der Neigung zum Neurotizismus bei den Kindern: Ergebnisse eines Längsschnittprojekts. *Psychologie in Erziehung und Unterricht, 56*, 85–94.

Rubin, D. B. (1987). *Multiple imputation for nonresponse in surveys.* New York: John Wiley & Sons.

Schafer, J. L., & Graham, J. W. (2002). Missing data: Our view of the state of the art. *Psychological Methods, 7*, 147–177.

Shek, D. T. L. (2000). Parental marital quality and well-being, parent–child relational quality, and Chinese adolescent adjustment. *The American Journal of Family Therapy, 28*, 147–162.

Sturaro, C., Denissen, J. J. A., van Aken, M. A. G., & Asendorpf, J. B. (2008). Person-environment transactions during emerging adulthood. *European Psychologist, 13*, 1–11.

Van Buuren, S., Brand, J. P. L., Groothuis-Oudshoorn, C. G. M., & Rubin, D. B. (2006). Fully conditional specification in multivariate imputation. *Journal of Statistical Computation and Simulation, 76*, 1049–1064.

Van Buuren, S., & Groothuis-Oudshoorn, K. (2011). Mice: Multivariate imputation by chained equations in R. *Journal of Statistical Software, 45,* 1–67.

Werneck, H., & Rollett, B. (2007). Der Einfluss elterlicher Partnerschaftsqualität auf Persönlichkeit und Bindungsrepräsentation der Kinder mit 11 Jahren. *Psychologie in Erziehung und Unterricht, 2,* 118–128.

Zhong-Hui, W., Hui-Lan, L., & Jian-Xin, Z. (2006). The relationship between parental rearing and adolescent personality traits. *Chinese Journal of Clinical Psychology, 14,* 315–317.

Intergenerational transmission of maternal and paternal parenting beliefs: The moderating role of interaction quality

Andrea B. Erzinger[1] and Andrea E. Steiger[2]

[1]Institute of Research on Teaching Profession and on Development of Competencies, University of Teacher Education St. Gallen, St. Gallen, Switzerland
[2]Institute of Psychology, University of Zurich, Zürich, Switzerland

The finding that values, attitudes, and behaviour can be transmitted across generations is long standing. However, the role of fathers in this process has been underinvestigated. Furthermore, many researchers have not tested moderation effects. We extended the literature by investigating *maternal and paternal* transmission of harsh parenting beliefs to their children 23 years later. Furthermore, we examined the *moderating role of interaction quality* and included gender and socioeconomic status as control variables. Our data were collected in a unique longitudinal study of 128 families across 23 years. We found high positive associations between the harsh parenting beliefs of parents and their adult children, but only the mother–child transmissions were moderated by interaction quality. Mothers pass on low levels as well as high levels of harsh parenting beliefs to their children if their interaction quality is poor. These findings highlight the importance of investigating intergenerational transmission in both mother–child and father–child dyads.

A large body of literature has revealed the intergenerational transmission of parenting behaviour and beliefs. These transmission effects hold for both problematic (Capaldi, Pears, Patterson, & Owen, 2003; Simons, Whitbeck, Conger, & Chyi-in, 1991) and positive parenting (Belsky, Jaffee, Sligo,

This publication is based on data from a research project funded by a grant (PMCDP1_129113) from the Swiss National Science Foundation (SNSF).

Woodward, & Silva, 2005; Chen & Kaplan, 2001) and for both parenting behaviour (Serbin & Karp, 2003) and parenting beliefs (van IJzendoorn, 1992). According to Chen and Kaplan (2001), most research in this field has focused on the consequences of parenting behaviour. Very little research has pointed out the role of cognitions in determining parenting behaviour (Simons, Beaman, Conger, & Chao, 1992). Since the 1980s, however, interest in parenting beliefs as an antecedent of parenting behaviour has increased notably. Beliefs about children's learning and discipline and concepts about the interplay of parenting and child development tend to be reflected in parenting behaviour. Research has shown that parenting behaviour links the parenting beliefs of parents with the beliefs of their children (Simons et al., 1992). Thus, to understand the transmission of parenting behaviours between generations, parenting beliefs must be considered. This longitudinal study addressed this issue by focusing on the intergenerational transmission of parenting beliefs.

FAMILIES AS THE PRIMARY SOURCE OF SOCIALIZATION

Families can be seen as the primary source of children's socialization because they influence children's development, values and attitudes (Grusec, Goodnow, & Kuczynski, 2000). Families transmit not only societal values and social norms but also more family-specific attitudes such as parenting styles and beliefs.

As Hofferth, Pleck, and Vesely (2012) indicate, almost no research has presented a methodologically rigorous test of the distinct role of fathering compared to mothering in cross-generational investigations of parenting patterns. To date, familial processes have been investigated by examining maternal influences almost exclusively (Thornberry, Freeman-Gallant, Lizotte, Krohn, & Smith, 2003; Vermulst, de Brock, & van Zutphen, 1991). However, more recent research has paid increasing attention to the father's role in the family, investigating the father's relevance to children's development (Lamb, 2010). Indeed, a small number of recent studies have shown that fathers transmit their parenting to the next generation and thus play an increasingly important role in intergenerational familial processes (Hofferth et al., 2012; Kitamura et al., 2009; Smith & Farrington, 2004). The importance of fathers is likely increasing as their role in the family has changed substantially during the past 10–20 years.

FATHERS AND HARSH PARENTING

The omission of fathers is particularly problematic when studying harsh parenting because research has revealed that fathers are significantly involved in violent parenting (Capaldi et al., 2003; Conger, Neppl, Kim, & Scaramella, 2003; Simons et al., 1991; Smith & Farrington, 2004). For example, in Simons et al.'s (1991) study, harsh parenting was directly transmitted to the sons of the next generation (G2), but the gender of the first generation (G1) did not play a role in this transmission process. Conversely, Smith and Farrington (2004) differentiated G1 mothers and fathers but investigated only G2 sons and therefore did not investigate transmission to G2 daughters. Their results, however, pointed in the same direction as outlined above. G2 sons who were poorly supervised by their parents in childhood showed inconsistent parenting behaviour as adults, inadequately supervising their own children to a higher degree than G2 sons who had not endured such poor parenting experiences in childhood. These findings highlight the importance of fathers and mothers in intergenerational transmission processes in families.

In research on the father's role in the transmission of harsh parenting, little attention has been given to the cognitions behind this parenting behaviour, despite the fact that beliefs have been shown to be important indicators of future parenting behaviour (Chen & Kaplan, 2001). The current study fills this gap by investigating mothers' and fathers' transmission of harsh parenting beliefs to their children.

DIRECT TRANSMISSION OF PARENTING BELIEFS

Among numerous theories that explain intrafamilial transmission processes of characteristics, behaviours, values and attitudes, Bandura's (1977) social learning theory is typically considered to provide the most accurate theoretical foundation (see Hofferth et al., 2012).

Social learning theory emphasizes the importance of parents as role-models, especially in early childhood. Parents act as role models for their children, who, in turn, learn parenting behaviours, attitudes and values through observation and imitation. Transmission occurs directly through practice, punishment or reinforcement (Bandura, 1977). Because families are the primary source of socialization in childhood, an emphasis on early parenting is crucial for testing transmission processes (Kovan, Chung, & Sroufe, 2009). Thus, this study focused on a sample of parents with young children who were in a sensitive period for parental influences.

To date, in addition to investigating direct transmission, research has often investigated *mediated* pathways. Various studies have reported indirect transmission via several mediators such as personality traits or behaviours (e.g., antisocial behaviour), positive relationships, conflicted marriages, or social participation in transmission processes (see e.g., Hofferth et al., 2012). However, less is known about *moderators* of intergenerational transmission processes of parenting (Conger, Belsky, & Capaldi, 2009).

MODERATORS OF INTERGENERATIONAL TRANSMISSION PROCESSES

Moderators in this context are potential sources of influence on the intergenerational transmission process of parenting behaviour or beliefs. They establish the context in which the intergenerational transmission occurs. Such knowledge is particularly informative for researchers or professionals in the field of familial relationships interested in promoting positive child rearing. With regard to moderators, research on the influence of gender on the transmission of parenting has shown inconsistent results (Belsky et al., 2005). Other studies that have investigated moderation effects have shown that positive parent–child relationships facilitate value transmission. Schönpflug (2001) found that value transmission in father–son relationships was strongest when fathers displayed an empathetic, less rigid parenting style. By contrast, Roest, Dubas, and Gerris (2009) found that a warm and close family climate increased the transmission of values only in the mother–child but not in the father–child dyad.

Grusec and Goodnow (1994) offered a rationale for testing for the moderating effect of parent–child relationship quality in value transmission research by explaining how values and behaviour are internalized. In their opinion, a prerequisite for adopting a parent's behaviour or beliefs is an *accurate* perception of the parent's position. This may be achieved by a nuanced and clear expression of the parent's view. Second, children need to accept or refuse the positions of their parents (Grusec & Goodnow, 1994). The likelihood that children will accept their parents' positions is higher if the family climate is warm and responsive. Therefore, high-quality interactions in parent–child relationships promote children's efforts to be more similar to their parents and to adopt their parents' positions (Grusec et al., 2000). Thus, a reasonable hypothesis would be that the intergenerational transmission of harsh parenting beliefs will change depending on the quality of the underlying parent–child relationship.

THE PRESENT STUDY

We used a unique data set from two generations measured across a time span of 23 years to investigate whether and how harsh parenting beliefs are transmitted across generations. Not only did we include three sources of information, but we were also able to avoid using retrospective reports by measuring parents' parenting beliefs when their children were 6 years old and then measuring the parenting beliefs of those children in adulthood.

Furthermore, we used identical measures of harsh parenting beliefs for the parents and the adult children 23 years later. According to Simons et al. (1991), it is crucial to differentiate between discipline and warmth when investigating parenting across generations. In line with this distinction, we focused more strongly on the aspect of discipline. More specifically, our study was concerned with harsh parenting beliefs, which we defined as demanding and controlling parenting characteristics. Parents with such characteristics show openness to punishment or discipline. Combined with rejecting, unresponsive and parent-centred characteristics, harsh parenting has been conceptualized as authoritarian power-asserting parenting (Baumrind, 1966, 1991; Maccoby & Martin, 1983).

Most importantly, we included maternal and paternal influences in our examination of transmission processes. Due to increasing societal changes with noticeable consequences not only for the individual but for the whole family, we argue that the focus of research should be shifted to a more integrative view of the family, including mothers *and* fathers in investigations of familial processes. This study extends the previous literature in several ways. We differentiated between mother–child and father–child dyads and used a balanced sample of fathers and mothers when testing the intergenerational transmission of harsh parenting beliefs. Based on prior research, we hypothesized that we would find cross-generational associations of harsh parenting beliefs in both dyads.

Second, to the best of our knowledge, no research has tested for interaction quality as a moderator when examining the transmission of *harsh parenting beliefs*. Therefore, we tested whether and how the quality of parent–child interactions would moderate the transmission of harsh parenting beliefs from one generation to the next. Based on prior research, we hypothesized that high interaction quality would increase the transmission of harsh parenting beliefs in both dyads.

METHOD

Sample

Randomly selected communal agencies in the German-speaking part of Switzerland were asked for the addresses of children who were expected to enroll in school in 1984. A total of 1035 parents of these children were contacted by mailed questionnaires; 445 parents (43%) returned the questionnaires in 1984. Although the sample was selected randomly, we must assume that there was a self-selection response bias. Some answers ($n = 65$) were excluded because no panel data could be gathered. Also, some respondents ($n = 16$) were excluded because they were missing all data for a particular construct or they turned in questionnaires with unreliable data (e.g., parents had answered questions together). After correcting the data for these issues, 193 mothers and 171 fathers out of 207 families took part in 1984. One year later, we conducted Wave 2, again by mailing questionnaires to the same families who had participated the year before. Maternal and paternal perceptions of their child's development in the first school year and the impact of school enrollment on selected aspects of parent–child relationships were investigated. In 1985, 194 mothers and 168 fathers of the initial 207 families participated in the study (Stöckli, 1989). More than 20 years later, we conducted Wave 3 by sending questionnaires to fathers, mothers and the adult children. In 2007, 76.8% of mothers and 68.1% of fathers of the initial 207 families took part in the study; 155 of the former children, who were then young adults, were interviewed as well (74.9% of the 207 families). The follow-up study in young adulthood examined educational pathways from childhood to adulthood as well as parent–child relationships across the lifespan. The final sample included 128 families that consisted of both the father and the mothers and one adult child who participated in this study (Wave 1, 1984: age$_{mother}$: $M = 35.35$, SD $= 3.92$; age$_{father}$: $M = 37.19$, SD $= 3.85$; age$_{child}$: $M = 6.62$, SD $= 0.49$) and children in young adulthood (Wave 3, 2007: age$_{child}$: $M = 29.14$, SD $= 0.49$); 51.6% ($n = 66$) of the children were female.

Measures

Harsh parenting beliefs. This scale consisted of three items (see Table 1 for item wordings and the results of a latent confirmatory factor analysis). It was originally created to measure teachers' attitudes towards discipline and control and was later adapted to the familial context (Konstanzer Fragebogen für Schul- und Erziehungseinstellungen (KSE) [Constance school and educational attitudes questionnaire]; Koch, Cloetta, & Müller-Fohrbrodt, 1972). Ratings were given on a Likert-type scale with higher values representing more control. The scale for mothers ($M = 3.19$, SD $= 0.85$, $\alpha = .71$) and fathers ($M = 3.34$, SD $= 0.82$, $\alpha = .68$) ranged from 1 to 5 and the scale for adult children from 1 to 6 ($M = 3.12$, SD $= 1.06$, $\alpha = .71$); internal consistencies were acceptable.

TABLE 1
Harsh parenting beliefs scale (Koch et al., 1972)

	German wording of the item	Translation of the item into English		Results of latent confirmatory factor analysis		
				Mother	Father	Adult child
1	Eine Ohrfeige zur rechten Zeit wirkt unter Umständen wie ein reinigendes Gewitter	A slap in the face at the right time will sometimes clear the air	Loading n_{Valid} $n_{Missing}$	.59*** 128[a] 0	.60*** 128[a] 0	.62*** 128 0
2	Bei den meisten Kindern muss man von Zeit zu Zeit einmal hart durch- greifen	With most children, harsh measures have to be taken occasionally	Loading n_{Valid} $n_{Missing}$	.92*** 128[a] 0	.75*** 128[a] 0	.73*** 127 1
3	Es tut den Kindern nur gut, wenn sie bereits in der Schule erfahren, dass man im Leben oft Dinge tun muss, an denen man keine Freude hat	It is for the children's benefit that they learn in school that we often have to do things in life that we do not like to do	Loading n_{Valid} $n_{Missing}$	.47*** 128[a] 0	.44*** 128[a] 0	.69*** 127 1

Note: For mothers and fathers, the scale ranges from 1(*very wrong*) to 5 (*very correct*) and for children from 1 (*strongly disagree*) to 6 (*strongly agree*).
[a] When missing, the 1984 data were imputed from the 1985 data.
***$p < .001$

54

Interaction quality. This scale consisted of four items (see Table 2 for item wordings and the results of a latent confirmatory factor analysis). Mothers and fathers indicated their perceptions of the quality of their interactions with their child (Stöckli, 1989). After reverse-coding negatively worded items, the scale for mothers ($M = 4.32$, SD $= 0.49$, $\alpha = .69$) and fathers ($M = 4.42$, SD $= 0.45$, $\alpha = .64$) ranged from 1 to 5 and showed acceptable internal consistency.

Socioeconomic status (SES). SES was measured with the Standard International Socio-Economic Index of Occupational Status (ISEI; Ganzeboom, De Graf, Treiman, & De Leeuw, 1992) for mothers ($M = 45.08$, SD $= 9.77$) and fathers ($M = 55.15$, SD $= 15.37$) separately. To represent family status, we chose the ISEI of the parent possessing the higher one ($M_{HISEI} = 56.03$; SD $= 13.74$; $n_{Missing} = 13$, 10.16%).

Analyses

We examined the research questions by applying latent structural equation modelling using Mplus (Muthén & Muthén, 1998–2010). If data on parents' harsh parenting beliefs were missing in 1984, they were imputed from the 1985 data. A high relative stability of parenting beliefs between these 2 years (not presented in this paper) justified this approach. Additionally, we used Full Information Maximum Likelihood (Kline, 2011) to estimate any data that were missing on the harsh parenting beliefs of the adult children in 2007 (see Tables 1 and 2).

TABLE 2
Interaction quality scale for fathers and mothers (Stockli, 1989)

	German wording of the item	*Translation of the item into English*		*Results of latent confirmatory factor analysis*	
				Mother	*Father*
1	Ich fühle mich durch das Kind gereizt, so dass ich verärgert bin	I get angry when I am irritated by my child	Loading n_{Valid} $n_{Missing}$	.54*** 128[a] 0	.46*** 128[a] 0
2	Ich bin stolz auf mein Kind	I am proud of my child	Loading n_{Valid} $n_{Missing}$	.82*** 128[a] 0	.56*** 128[a] 0
3	Ich bin von meinem Kind enttäuscht	I am disappointed with my child	Loading n_{Valid} $n_{Missing}$	.57*** 128[a] 0	.53*** 128[a] 0
4	Mein Kind macht mir Freude	I enjoy being with my child	Loading n_{Valid} $n_{Missing}$	.55*** 128[a] 0	.73*** 128[a] 0

Note: The scale ranges from 1 (*always or almost always*) to 5 (*never or almost never*).
[a] When missing, the 1984 data were imputed from the 1985 data.
***$p < .001$

We included child's gender and SES as control variables in our analyses. Although often neglected in prior research, family SES explains similarities between generations. We therefore integrated this variable as a control (Serbin & Karp, 2003; Simons et al., 1991; van IJzendoorn, 1992).

First, we tested a latent structural equation model for the transmission of parenting beliefs in mother–child and father–child dyads controlling for child's gender and family SES in childhood (see Table 4, Models 1 and 2). We followed a step-up approach to test for measurement invariance across time (Brown, 2006). Partial strong factorial invariance was established.

Finally, we tested a latent structural equation model that predicted adult children's harsh parenting beliefs from their parents' harsh parenting beliefs more than two decades later as well as the parents' self-reported quality of interactions with their child in childhood. We tested this model for both the mother–child (see Table 5, Model 4A) and father–child dyads (see Table 6, Model 5A). We also controlled for family SES in childhood and for the child's gender (see Table 5, Model 4B, and Table 6, Model 5B). All these models showed good model fit.

We tested the interaction of parental harsh parenting beliefs and the quality of the parent–child interaction on the adult children's harsh parenting beliefs to test our hypothesis that interaction quality would moderate the transmission of harsh parenting beliefs between generations. Mplus offers the latent moderated structural equations method (Klein & Moosbrugger, 2000) to test for interactions. This method provides the advantage that normal distributions are assumed for latent independent variables and error variables, and no product indicator term has to be produced. Furthermore, the nonnormality of the latent product term is taken into account (Klein & Moosbrugger, 2000). Regular model fit indices are not provided in Mplus (Wang & Wang, 2012) because the calculation of the χ^2 goodness-of-fit test requires a saturated model that cannot be computed. Mplus computes only unstandardized solutions. To obtain standardized results, the manifest indicators of the latent independent variables and the dependent variable were z-transformed. Standardized path coefficients are useful, particularly for investigating the relative impact of the predictors (Henseler & Fassott, 2010).

RESULTS

For the descriptive statistics of the constructs, see Table 3.

To analyse the transmission of harsh parenting beliefs, we first tested mother–child and father–child dyads. Latent structural equation modelling showed that harsh parenting beliefs were significantly transmitted from mother to child ($\beta = .33$, $p = .004$). After controlling for child's gender and family SES, transmission in the mother–child dyad was still significant ($\beta = .28$, $p = .002$; see Table 4, Models 1A and 1B). Furthermore, fathers

TABLE 3
Correlations, means and variances among the manifest scales and moderators

Variable	1	2	3	4	5	6	7
1. Child's gender		<.01	.10	−.08	.18*	−.04	−.08
2. Family's SES in childhood t1			−.10	−.10	−.14	<.01	−.02
3. Mother's harsh parenting beliefs t1/t2				.49***	.23**	−.16+	−.01
4. Father's harsh parenting beliefs t1/t2					.19*	−.06	.02
5. Adult child's harsh parenting beliefs t3						−.22*	−.14
6. Mother's interaction quality t1/t2							.40***
7. Father's interaction quality t1/t2							
n_{Valid}	128	115	128	128	128	128	128
$n_{Missing}$	0	13	0	0	0	0	0
Mean		56.03	3.19	3.34	3.12	4.26	4.35
Variance		188.91	.73	.68	1.12	.23	.17

$^{+}p < .10$, $^{*}p < .05$, $^{**}p < .01$, $^{***}p < .001$.

significantly transmitted their parenting beliefs to their child ($\beta = .35$, $p = .004$). This significant association still held after controlling for child's gender and family SES ($\beta = .35$, $p = .005$; see Table 4 Models 2A and 2B). The child's gender influenced the adult children's parenting beliefs ($\beta = .20$, $p = .054$; $\beta = .27$, $p = .008$) such that men showed more harsh parenting beliefs than women (see Table 4, Models 1B and 2B).

After the moderator interaction quality was introduced, mothers still transmitted harsh parenting beliefs to their child ($\beta = .34$, $p = .003$) across a time period of more than two decades (see Table 5, Model 4A). This transmission decreased slightly ($\beta = .33$, $p = .004$) after controlling for child's gender and family SES in childhood (see Table 5, Model 4B). The same association was found for father–child dyads: fathers passed on their harsh parenting beliefs to their child after the moderator interaction quality was added to the model ($\beta = .36$, $p = .004$; see Table 6, Model 5A). This association held after controlling for child's gender and family SES in childhood ($\beta = .39$, $p = .003$; see Table 6, Model 5B). The quality of mothers' interactions with their child did not significantly influence adult children's harsh parenting beliefs (see Table 5, all models). There was a tendency for father–child interaction quality to negatively influence children's harsh parenting beliefs ($\beta = -.21$, $p = .096$; see Table 6), indicating that the children of fathers who had better quality father–child interactions showed lower levels of harsh parenting beliefs two decades later. However, this result did not hold after controlling for both control variables

TABLE 4
Transmission of harsh parenting beliefs between fathers, mothers and adult children

Variable	Model 1A	Model 1B	Model 2A	Model 2B
Transmission of mother's harsh parenting beliefs on adult child's harsh parenting beliefs (stand. est. (se))	.33** (.11)	.28* (.12)		
Transmission of father's harsh parenting beliefs on adult child's harsh parenting beliefs (stand. est. (se))			.35** (.12)	.35** (.13)
Influence of child's gender on mother's/father's harsh parenting beliefs (stand. est. (se))		.08 (.11)		−.10 (.11)
Influence of family's SES on mother's/father's harsh parenting beliefs (stand. est. (se))		−.11 (.11)		−.10 (.11)
Influence of child's gender on adult child's harsh parenting beliefs (stand. est. (se))		.20⁺ (.11)		.27** (.10)
Influence of family's SES on adult child's harsh parenting beliefs (stand. est. (se))		−.12 (.11)		−.12 (.11)
Correlation ($r_{Pearson}$) of mother's and father's harsh parenting beliefs				
Explained variance (R^2) of adult child's harsh parenting beliefs	.11	.15	.12	.20
AIC	2307	2093	2313	2089
BIC	2361	2156	2367	2152
ABIC	2301	2084	2307	2079
χ^2 (df)	5.01 (8)	14.36 (16)	12.09 (8)	23.39 (16)
p	.757	.572	.147	.104
RMSEA (CI)	<.001 (<.001/.073)	<.001 (<.001/.078)	.063 (<.001/.131)	.063 (<.001/.115)
CFI	1.000	1.000	.971	.947

Notes: Model 1: Mother–child dyad (partial strong factorial measurement invariance over time). Model 2: Father–child dyad (partial strong factorial measurement invariance over time). AIC = Akaike Information Criteria; BIC = Bayesian Information Criteria; ABIC = Adjusted Bayesian Information Criteria; RMSEA = Root Mean Square Error of Approximation; CFI = Comparative Fit Index.
⁺$p < .10$, *$p < .05$, **$p < .01$

TABLE 5

Transmission of harsh parenting beliefs between mothers and adult children: The moderating role of maternal interaction quality

	Model 4A	Model 4B	Model 4C	Model 4D
Transmission of mother's harsh parenting beliefs on adult child's harsh parenting beliefs (stand. est. (se))	.34** (.11)	.33** (.12)	.38* (.17)	.38* (.18)
Influence of mother's interaction quality on adult child's harsh parenting beliefs (stand. est. (se))	−.10 ns (.12)	−.12 ns (.13)	−.11 ns (.17)	−.09 ns (.17)
Influence of the interaction of mother's harsh parenting beliefs and interaction quality on adult child's harsh parenting beliefs (stand. est. (se))			−.33+ (.18)	−.37* (.18)
Influence of child's gender on mother's harsh parenting beliefs (stand. est. (se))		−.04 ns (.11)		−.01 ns (.19)
Influence of family's SES on mother's harsh parenting beliefs (stand. est. (se))		<.06 ns (.11)		<.01 ns (<.01)
Influence of child's gender on mother's interaction quality (stand. est. (se))		−.09 ns (.11)		−.09 ns (.21)
Influence of family's SES on mother's interaction quality (stand. est. (se))		−.15 ns (.11)		<.01 ns (<.01)
Influence of child's gender on adult child's harsh parenting beliefs (stand. est. (se))		.23* (.10)		.85* (.33)
Influence of family's SES on adult child's harsh parenting beliefs (stand. est. (se))		−.14 ns (.10)		<.01 ns (.01)
Correlation ($r_{Pearson}$) of mother's and father's harsh parenting beliefs	−.20+ (.11)	−.19 ns (.12)	−.17+ (.11)	−.18+ (.11)
Explained variance (R^2) of adult child's harsh parenting beliefs	.14+	.21*		

(continued)

TABLE 5 – continued

	Model 4A	Model 4B	Model 4C	Model 4D
AIC	3405	3076	4617	4620
BIC	3496	3180	4711	4731
ABIC	3395	3060	4607	4608
χ^2 (df)	30.38 (33)	51.00 (47)		
p	.598	.319		
RMSEA (CI)	<.001 (<.001/.058)	.027 (<.001/.069)		
CFI	1.000	.982		

Notes: Model 4: Mother–child dyad (partial strong factorial measurement invariance between mother's and adult child's harsh parenting beliefs). A: model without interaction effect, not controlled for SES and child's gender. B: model without interaction effect, controlled for SES and child's gender. C: model with interaction effect, not controlled for SES and child's gender. D: model with interaction effect, controlled for SES and child's gender. AIC = Akaike Information Criteria; BIC = Bayesian Information Criteria; ABIC = Adjusted Bayesian Information Criteria; RMSEA = Root Mean Square Error of Approximation; CFI = Comparative Fit Index.

$^+p < .10$, $^*p < .05$, $^{**}p < .01$

TABLE 6

Transmission of harsh parenting beliefs between fathers and adult children: The moderating role of paternal interaction quality

	Model 5A Stand. est. (se)	Model 5B Stand. est. (se)	Model 5C Stand. est. (se)	Model 5D Stand. est. (se)
Transmission of father's on adult child's harsh parenting beliefs (stand. est. (se))	.36** (.12)	.39** (.13)	.41* (.19)	.43* (.19)
Influence of father's interaction quality on adult child's harsh parenting beliefs (stand. est. (se))	−.21[+] (.12)	−.19 ns (.13)	−.20 ns (.17)	−.19 ns (.17)
Influence of the interaction of father's harsh parenting beliefs and interaction quality (stand. est. (se))			−.20 ns (.20)	−.19 ns (.19)
Influence of child's gender on father's harsh parenting beliefs (stand. est. (se))		−.03 ns (.12)		−.07 ns (.22)
Influence of family's SES on father's harsh parenting beliefs (stand. est. (se))		−.09 ns (.12)		<.01 ns (<.01)
Influence of child's gender on father's interaction quality (stand. est. (se))		−.08 ns (.11)		−.08 ns (.22)
Influence of family's SES on father's interaction quality (stand. est. (se))		−.11 ns (.11)		<.01 ns (<.01)
Influence of child's gender on adult child's harsh parenting beliefs (stand. est. (se))		.25* (.10)		.77* (.31)
Influence of family's SES on adult child's harsh parenting beliefs (stand. est. (se))		−.13 ns (.11)		<.01 ns (<.01)
Correlation ($r_{Pearson}$) of mother's and father's harsh parenting beliefs	.02 ns (.14)	.02 ns (.14)	.01 ns (.13)	.01 ns (.13)
Explained variance (R^2) of adult child's harsh parenting beliefs	.17[+]	.27*		

(continued)

TABLE 6 – *continued*

	Model 5A *Stand. est. (se)*	Model 5B *Stand. est. (se)*	Model 5C *Stand. est. (se)*	Model 5D *Stand. est. (se)*
AIC	3384	3066	4679	4682
BIC	3475	3170	4773	4794
ABIC	3374	3050	4669	4670
$\chi 2$ (*df*)	35.24 (33)	55.49 (47)		
p	.363	.185		
RMSEA (CI)	.023 (<.001/.070)	.040 (<.001/.076)		
CFI	.988	.955		

Notes: Model 5: Father–child dyad (partial strong factorial measurement invariance between father's and adult child's harsh parenting beliefs). A: model without interaction effect, not controlled for SES and child's gender. B: model without interaction effect, controlled for SES and child's gender. C: model with interaction effect, not controlled for SES and child's gender. D: model with interaction effect, controlled for SES and child's gender. AIC = Akaike Information Criteria; BIC = Bayesian Information Criteria; ABIC = Adjusted Bayesian Information Criteria; RMSEA = Root Mean Square Error of Approximation; CFI = Comparative Fit Index.

$^{+}p < .10$, $^{*}p < .05$, $^{**}p < .01$

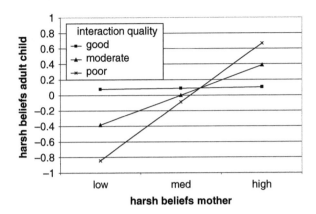

Figure 1. Transmission of harsh parenting beliefs moderated by interaction quality.

(see Table 6, Model 5B). There was a tendency for mothers' harsh parenting beliefs to be negatively associated with mother–child interaction quality ($r = -.20$, $p = .065$; see Table 5, Model 4A), but fathers' harsh parenting beliefs were not correlated with father–child interaction quality (see Table 6, all models). In young adulthood, sons showed harsh parenting beliefs to a significantly higher extent than daughters (see all models).

We tested the moderating role of parent–child interaction quality. The interaction of mothers' harsh parenting beliefs and the quality of maternal interactions with the child had a significantly negative influence on the harsh parenting beliefs of the adult child ($\beta = -.37$, $p = .042$) after controlling for child's gender and family SES in childhood (see Table 5, Model 4D).

In relationships characterized by high-quality interactions, the transmission of harsh parenting beliefs between mothers and their children occurred to a smaller extent, and vice versa, mothers were more likely to pass on their harsh parenting beliefs in poor-quality relationships. Thus, if mother–child interaction quality was high, *children's parenting beliefs were independent of mothers' parenting beliefs.* That is, under conditions of high-quality interactions, we did not see a *specific transmission pattern.* On the other hand, children's harsh parenting beliefs seemed to be rooted in the mothers' parenting beliefs if mother–child interaction quality was poor (see Figure 1).

The main effect of interaction quality did not reach significance, a finding that indicates that interaction quality becomes relevant only in conjunction with harsh parenting beliefs. The interaction between fathers' harsh parenting beliefs and interaction quality did not significantly affect the harsh parenting beliefs of the adult children ($\beta = -.19$, $p = .324$; see Table 6, Model 5D). Thus, the

63

transmission of harsh parenting beliefs in father–child dyads did not depend on the quality of this relationship.

DISCUSSION

Traditionally, previous research on intergenerational transmission of parenting beliefs and behaviours has focused on mothers. However, some studies have revealed that fathers are often involved in negative parenting patterns and that they are likely to pass on these negative patterns to their children. Therefore, many researchers have called for a closer investigation of the role of fathers in families. We aimed to fill this research gap by investigating both maternal and paternal transmission effects of harsh parenting beliefs. We found a positive association between parenting beliefs of the first and second generations, even after controlling for SES and gender. Harsh parenting beliefs are still transmitted to children more than two decades later. These findings correspond with recent results on transmission processes found for mothers (Belsky et al., 2005), for fathers (Smith & Farrington, 2004), or for both (Kitamura et al., 2009; Simons et al., 1992).

Additionally, we tested the moderating role of interaction quality in mother–child and father–child dyads. Our moderator was consequential only for mother–child but not for father–child dyads. High-quality interactions between mothers and their children did not moderate the transmission of harsh parenting beliefs; that is, if mothers had a good interaction style with their children, children seemed to be "unaffected" by the parenting beliefs of their mothers. It could be that mothers with high interaction quality *and* high harsh parenting beliefs did not need to act upon their harsh parenting beliefs. Furthermore, it could be that children who were fortunate to have good-quality interactions with their parents were encouraged to form their own opinions on parenting. This, in turn, could explain why these children did not simply adopt harsh parenting beliefs but developed a variety of parenting beliefs independent of their parents' beliefs.

On the other hand, poor maternal interaction quality led to an increased transmission in both directions: Low and high levels of mothers' harsh parenting beliefs were transmitted to their children. It could be that poor interaction quality did not encourage children to question and reflect on their mothers' parenting beliefs but led to an unscrutinized adoption of their mothers' positions. Mothers with harsh parenting beliefs might be more likely to practice harsh discipline with their children. Because actual maternal behaviour may be strongly related to mothers' interaction quality, mothers with high levels of harsh parenting beliefs were more likely to have poor-quality interactions with their children.

Contrary to our results, research on the transmission of values has found that warm parent–child relationships promote the transmission of hedonistic values in mother–child dyads (Roest et al., 2009). Our study showed only a moderating effect of poor interaction quality in mother–child dyads. In line with our results, Roest et al. (2009) found that transmission in father–child dyads did not increase with warmer family interactions.

Another explanation for our finding of moderation effects on transmission only in mother–child dyads might be due to the fact that our investigation began in the early 1980s. At that time, the role of men and women were much more strongly prescribed than today such that mothers were expected to invest more heavily in the family than fathers. Therefore, it would be reasonable to assume that mothers in our study may have cultivated the quality of their interactions with their children more than fathers did. Today, the father's role in family interactions is changing; therefore, we assume that this accounts for the moderating effect on father–child transmission processes found in more recent research (see e.g., Schönpflug, 2001). Very few studies have compared transmission in mother–child and father–child dyads. For example, Smith and Farrington (2004) found that fathers but not mothers pass on poor supervision to their children. Similarly, Hofferth et al. (2012) found a direct association between G1 and G2 positive fathering. However, Simons et al. (1991) found the opposite result, that is, the transmission of harsh parenting in mother–child but not in father–child dyads. Contrary to these studies, we found associations between children's and parents' harsh parenting beliefs for both dyads. Considering these inconsistent findings, future studies should more strongly emphasize the role of fathers in families and test for both maternal *and* paternal transmission, particularly with respect to poor parenting.

Limitations

This study has several advantages compared to earlier studies on the transmission of parenting. However, one limitation of this study includes the small sample size. First, we suspect that some of the nonsignificant results may be a result of low statistical power. Second, the small sample size did not allow us to interpret the results in a common model for fathers and mothers. To compare maternal and paternal transmission, future research should aim to integrate fathers and mothers in a common model. Finally, the limited sample size did not permit separate analyses for sons and daughters, although previous research determined that child's gender was another potential moderator. Furthermore, we found only very small associations. Considering the long time span of over 20 years, however, small effects are usually considered as relevant (Chen & Kaplan, 2001). Furthermore, we focused solely on *direct* transmission paths, excluding possible indirect transmission processes.

CONCLUSION

In summary, this study contributes to the literature in several ways. We found clear associations between harsh parenting beliefs of parents and their children. Furthermore, we tested interaction quality as an important moderator of transmission processes. We found that poor interaction quality in mother–child dyads fostered the transmission of both low and high levels of mothers' harsh parenting beliefs.

This study emphasizes an integrative view of family, investigating the roles of both mothers and fathers in families. Future research in this field should always include fathers as their familial role has changed substantially since the 1980s. Thus, this study also contributes to a better understanding of intergenerational transmission processes of parenting beliefs in fathers and mothers and has implications for researchers and practitioners working in the field of child development and family.

REFERENCES

Bandura, A. (1977). *Social learning theory*. Englewood Cliffs, NJ: Prentice-Hall.

Baumrind, D. (1966). Effects of authoritative parental control on child behavior. *Child Development, 37*, 887–907. Retrieved from http://www.jstor.org/stable/1126611

Baumrind, D. (1991). The influence of parenting style on adolescent competence and substance use. *The Journal of Early Adolescence, 11*, 56–95. doi:10.1177/0272431691111004

Belsky, J., Jaffee, S. R., Sligo, J., Woodward, L., & Silva, P. A. (2005). Intergenerational transmission of warm-sensitive-stimulating parenting: A prospective study of mothers and fathers of 3-year-olds. *Child Development, 76*, 384–396. doi:10.1111/j.1467-8624.2005.00852.x

Brown, T. A. (2006). *Confirmatory factor analysis for applied research. Methodology in the social sciences*. New York, NY: Guilford Press.

Capaldi, D. M., Pears, K. C., Patterson, G. R., & Owen, L. D. (2003). Continuity of parenting practices across generations in an at-risk sample: A prospective comparison of direct and mediated associations. *Journal of Abnormal Child Psychology, 31*, 127–142. doi:10.1023/A:1022518123387

Chen, Z.-Y., & Kaplan, H. B. (2001). Intergenerational transmission of constructive parenting. *Journal of Marriage and Family, 63*, 17–31. doi:10.1111/j.1741-3737.2001.00017.x

Conger, R. D., Belsky, J., & Capaldi, D. M. (2009). The intergenerational transmission of parenting: Closing comments for the special section. *Developmental Psychology, 45*, 1276–1283. doi: 10.1037/a0016911

Conger, R. D., Neppl, T., Kim, K. J., & Scaramella, L. (2003). Angry and aggressive behavior across three generations: A prospective, longitudinal study of parents and children. *Journal of Abnormal Child Psychology, 31*, 143–160. doi:10.1023/A:1022570107457

Ganzeboom, H. B. G., De Graf, P. M., Treiman, D. J., & De Leeuw, J. (1992). A standard international socio-economic index of occupational status. *Social Science Research, 21*, 1–56. Retrieved from http://home.fsw.vu.nl/hbg.ganzeboom/Pdf/1992-ganzeboom-degraaf-treiman-isei68-%28ssr%29.pdf

Grusec, J. E., & Goodnow, J. (1994). Impact of parental discipline methods on the child's internalization of values: A reconceptualization of current points of view. *Developmental Psychology, 30*, 4–19. doi:10.1037/0012-1649.30.1.4

Grusec, J. E., Goodnow, J. J., & Kuczynski, L. (2000). New directions in analyses of parenting contributions to children's acquisition of values. *Child Development, 71*, 205–211. doi:10.1111/1467-8624.00135

Henseler, J., & Fassott, G. (2010). Testing moderating effects in PLS path models: An illustration of available procedures. In V. Esposito Vinzi (Ed.), *Handbook of partial least squares* (pp. 713–735). Berlin: Springer.

Hofferth, S. L., Pleck, J. H., & Vesely, C. K. (2012). The transmission of parenting from fathers to sons. *Parenting, 12*, 282–305. doi:10.1080/15295192.2012.709153

Kitamura, T., Shikai, N., Uji, M., Hiramura, H., Tanaka, N., & Shono, M. (2009). Intergenerational transmission of parenting style and personality: Direct influence or mediation? *Journal of Child and Family Studies, 18*, 541–556. doi:10.1007/s10826-009-9256-z

Klein, A., & Moosbrugger, H. (2000). Maximum likelihood estimation of latent interaction effects with the LMS method. *Psychometrika, 65*, 457–474. doi:10.1007/BF02296338

Kline, R. B. (2011). *Principles and practice of structural equation modeling* (3rd ed.). New York, NY: Guilford Press.

Koch, J. J., Cloetta, B., & Müller-Fohrbrodt, G. (1972). *Konstanzer Fragebogen für Schul- und Erziehungseinstellungen KSE* [Constance school and educational attitudes questionnaire]. Weinheim: Beltz Test.

Kovan, N. M., Chung, A. L., & Sroufe, L. A. (2009). The intergenerational continuity of observed early parenting: A prospective, longitudinal study. *Developmental Psychology, 45*, 1205–1213. doi:10.1037/a0016542

Lamb, M. E. (Ed.). (2010). *The role of the father in child development* (5th ed). Hoboken, NJ: Wiley.

Maccoby, E. E., & Martin, J. A. (1983). Socialization in the context of the family: Parent–child interaction. In P. H. Mussen & E. M. Hetherington (Eds.), *Handbook of child psychology* (Vol. 4, 4th ed.) (pp. 1–101). New York, NY: Wiley.

Muthén, L. K., & Muthén, B. O. (1998–2010). *Mplus user's guide* (6th ed.). Los Angeles, CA: Muthén & Muthén.

Roest, A. M. C., Dubas, J. S., & Gerris, J. R. M. (2009). Value transmissions between fathers, mothers, and adolescent and emerging adult children: The role of the family climate. *Journal of Family Psychology, 23*, 146–155. doi:10.1037/a0015075

Schönpflug, U. (2001). Intergenerational transmission of values. *Journal of Cross-Cultural Psychology, 32*, 174–185. doi:10.1177/0022022101032002005

Serbin, L., & Karp, J. (2003). Intergenerational studies of parenting and the transfer of risk from parent to child. *Current Directions in Psychological Science, 12*, 138–142. Retrieved from. http://www.jstor.org/stable/20182860

Simons, R. L., Beaman, J., Conger, R. D., & Chao, W. (1992). Gender differences in the intergenerational transmission of parenting beliefs. *Journal of Marriage and Family, 54*, 823–836. Retrieved from http://www.jstor.org/stable/353164

Simons, R. L., Whitbeck, L. B., Conger, R. D., & Chyi-in, W. (1991). Intergenerational transmission of harsh parenting. *Developmental Psychology, 27*, 159–171. doi:10.1037/0012-1649.27.1.159

Smith, C. A., & Farrington, D. P. (2004). Continuities in antisocial behavior and parenting across three generations. *Journal of Child Psychology and Psychiatry, 45*, 230–247. doi:10.1111/j.1469-7610.2004.00216.x

Stöckli, G. (1989). *Vom Kind zum Schüler: Zur Veränderung der Eltern-Kind-Beziehung am Beispiel "Schuleintritt"* [From child to student. Change of parent–child relationship by school entrance]. Bad Heilbrunn: Klinkhardt.

Thornberry, T. P., Freeman-Gallant, A., Lizotte, A. J., Krohn, M. D., & Smith, C. A. (2003). Linked lives: The intergenerational transmission of antisocial behavior. *Journal of Abnormal Child Psychology, 31*, 171–184. doi:10.1023/A:1022574208366

van IJzendoorn, M. H. (1992). Intergenerational transmission of parenting: A review of studies in nonclinical populations. *Developmental Review, 12*, 76–99. doi:10.1016/0273-2297(92)90004-L

Vermulst, A. A., de Brock, A. J. L. L., & van Zutphen, R. A. H. (1991). Transmission of parenting across generations. In P. K. Smith (Ed.), *The psychology of grandparenthood* (pp. 100–122). London: Routledge.

Wang, J., & Wang, X. (2012). *Structural equation modeling: Applications using Mplus*. Chichester: Wiley.

Parents' depressive symptoms and children's adjustment over time are mediated by parenting, but differentially for fathers and mothers

Dorothea E. Dette-Hagenmeyer and Barbara Reichle

Institute of Psychology and Sociology, Ludwigsburg University of Education, Ludwigsburg, Germany

Parenting has been found to act as a mediator of the relation between parents' depressive symptoms and children's adjustment. The present study replicated this result, and also found specific effects of gender for both parents and children. A total of 319 parents provided reports of their depressive symptoms (BDI) and two parenting styles (APQ; inconsistent discipline and positive parenting) as well as of their elementary schoolchildren's adjustment (VBV-EL; oppositional-defiant behaviour, hyperactivity, internalizing, social-emotional competence). The first and second measurement occasions were six months apart. Bivariate correlations showed the expected pattern of positive associations between parental depression, child maladjustment and problematic parenting. However, the results differed for mothers and fathers, and the mediation was moderated by the children's gender. Inconsistent discipline was a mediator for both fathers and mothers. The path from fathers' depression was additionally negatively mediated by positive parenting. Boys were more vulnerable than girls.

Parents' depressive symptoms have been shown to have a significant negative effect on adjustment for children and adolescents (for reviews, see Cummings & Davies, 1994; Goodman & Gotlib, 1999). Problem behaviours such as internalizing and externalizing were higher in children of depressed parents (e.g., mothers' symptoms of depression were associated with adolescents' externalizing behaviours; Kouros & Garber, 2010), and a recent three-year longitudinal study revealed that mothers' depressive symptoms were associated with their elementary schoolchildren's lower ability to regulate emotions

(Blandon, Calkins, Keane, & O'Brien, 2008). Most studies have focused on mothers, and only a few have analyzed data from fathers. Some of these studies found similar results for fathers with a significant association between fathers' depression and children's adjustment (see Kane & Garber, 2004). Others, however, reported different results for fathers: For instance, fathers' but not mothers' depressive symptoms predicted children's externalizing symptoms over time, whereas mothers' but not fathers' depressive symptoms predicted children's internalizing symptoms over time (Cummings, Schermerhorn, Keller, & Davies, 2008). However, there are too few studies to draw conclusions about the role of parents' gender in the link between parents' depressive symptoms and children's adjustment at this time.

One way to explore this further is to study moderators and mediators of this link. After discovering *that* parental depression influences children's adjustment, researchers began to ask *how* this influence is exerted. Several studies have examined the mechanism behind the relation between parents' depressed mood and children's adjustment. An integrative model by Goodman and Gotlib (1999) assumes four mechanisms: (1) heritability, (2) dysfunctional neuroregulatory mechanisms, (3) negative maternal cognitions, behaviour, and affect, and (4) exposure to a stressful environment. The third path assumes that parental depression results in specific parenting behaviour, which in turn influences children's behaviour and children's adjustment. Goodman and Gotlib proposed exposure to mothers' negative and/or maladaptive cognitions, behaviours and affect as one of the potential mechanisms for the transmission of risk to the children of depressed mothers. In other words, mothers' depression-related deficient parenting is one possible mediator of the detrimental relation between parental depression and children's adjustment.

This mediation hypothesis can be tested by assessing (1) whether depressive symptoms predict parenting and (2) whether parenting impacts children's adjustment.

PARENTAL DEPRESSIVE SYMPTOMS AND PARENTING

The link between parental depressive symptoms and parenting has been shown in several studies. Mothers with depressive symptoms showed lower levels of firm and consistent, warm and nurturing and positive discipline behaviour (Letourneau, Salmani, & Duffett-Leger, 2010). Over time, mothers with depressive symptoms more often even exhibited decreases in their positive parenting (high warmth and support, low rejection and control; Waylen & Stewart-Brown, 2010). Children of mothers with postpartum depression showed lower cognitive performance and more behavioural problems (Laucht, Esser, & Schmidt, 2002). A meta-analysis found that depressed mothers perceived more difficulties with child rearing and also had numerous parenting difficulties. A moderate positive association was found between maternal depression and negative parenting behaviour, a small to moderate positive association with disengaged behaviour, and a small negative association with positive interactions (Lovejoy, Graczyk, O'Hare, & Neuman, 2000). Again, as for the relation between parents' depression and children's adjustment, most of these studies have reported data for mothers only. Wilson and Durbin (2010), however, found similar results for fathers in their meta-analysis. Paternal depression had small but significant effects on parenting, with depressed fathers enacting decreases in positive and increases in negative parenting behaviours.

PARENTING AND CHILDREN'S ADJUSTMENT

The link between parenting practices and child behaviour or children's adjustment has been shown in many studies. Authoritative parenting—characterized by high warmth, control and autonomy support—has been linked to positive child development in cognitive and social-emotional domains (Baumrind, 1993; Laible & Carlo, 2004). Mothers with more inconsistent parenting had sons with more antisocial behaviour, relationship problems and school problems (Conger, Patterson, & Ge, 1995). This was also found over time: high parental engagement and low frequencies of harsh discipline were related to low levels of externalizing behaviour in elementary schoolchildren three years later (Beelmann, Stemmler, Lösel, & Jaursch, 2007). A meta-analysis found a significant association between parental caregiving—"approval, guidance, motivational strategies, synchrony and absence of coercive control"—and children's externalizing behaviour (Rothbaum & Weisz, 1994, p. 66).

Here, too, the focus has been on mother-child dyads. Only recently has research begun to include fathers, but studies have shown that the genders of both the parent and the child moderate the relation between parenting and the children's outcomes. Perceived rigid control from mothers but not from fathers was associated with lower levels of perceived social competence in adolescents (Laible & Carlo, 2004). High parental involvement and inconsistent discipline were related to lower aggressive behaviour in girls but not in boys (Koglin & Petermann, 2008). A meta-analysis found gender differences between boys and girls with stronger links for preadolescent boys and their mothers (Rothbaum & Weisz, 1994). One study that tested the generality of the links between parenting practices and children's adjustment found that only parent gender, child gender and family structure significantly moderated the relation between parenting and children's adjustment (Amato & Fowler, 2002). No overall interaction was found for race, ethnicity, education or income with regard to the relation between parenting and children's adjustment. The association between harsh punishment and children's behavioural problems was stronger for mothers than for fathers and also stronger for sons than for daughters. In sum, evidence of the different relations between mothers' and fathers' caregiving and sons' and daughters' adjustment has been mixed; thus, we also addressed this question in the present study.

MEDIATION MODELS

After finding that parenting is related to children's adjustment and that parental depressive symptoms are related to both parenting and children's adjustment, some studies directly tested for mediators of the relation between parents' depressive symptoms and children's adjustment in order to identify the specific behaviours of depressed parents that lead to children's maladjustment. In a nonclinical sample, the link between parents' depressive symptoms and children's internalizing problems was mediated by parental rejection and parental monitoring, the link between parents' depressive symptoms and children's externalizing problems was mediated by parental nurturance and parental rejection, and the link between parents' depressive symptoms and children's prosocial behaviour was mediated by parental nurturance and parental monitoring (Elgar, Mills, McGrath, Waschbusch, & Brownridge, 2007). However, no distinction was made between mothers' and fathers' parenting. Another mediator of the link between mothers' depressive symptoms and sons' adolescent problem behaviour was the level of family conflict (Burt et al., 2005). The relation between parents' depressive symptoms and children's externalizing problems was mediated by positive parenting (Parent et al., 2010). In a clinical sample, maternal depression and maternal parenting (laxness, overreactivity, verbosity) were related to children's internal and external problems (Herwig, Wirtz, & Bengel, 2004). Also, maladaptive parenting mediated not only the effect of parents' depression on children's adjustment but also the effect of mothers' negative and positive affect on children's problem behaviour (Karazsia & Wildman, 2009). Again, however, longitudinal studies that have compared mothers' and fathers' effect as well as studies that have tested for children's gender as a moderator are scarce: all of the aforementioned studies either analyzed data from one parent only or did not differentiate parent gender and rather assumed that the model was the same for mothers and fathers. The current study was designed to address this question.

THE CURRENT STUDY

The current study was based on longitudinal dyadic data and was designed to disentangle parent and child gender in these mediation models. The analytic techniques that we employed allowed for the dependent nature of our dyadic data. We addressed whether parenting style mediates the link between parents' depressive symptoms and children's adjustment and whether the effects are the same for mothers and fathers and boys and girls. We hypothesized that (H1) the relation between parents' depressive symptoms and children's externalizing and internalizing behaviours as well as children's social competence would be mediated by inconsistent and (a lack of) positive parenting styles. We expected differences in signs for different parenting styles and levels of children's adjustment. Specifically, we expected positive correlations between inconsistent parenting and children's

71

internalizing and externalizing behaviours as well as between positive parenting and children's social competence. We expected negative correlations between inconsistent parenting and children's social competence as well as between positive parenting and children's internalizing and externalizing behaviours. Also, we expected (H2) that mothers' and fathers' models would differ. Based on previous results (Amato & Fowler, 2002; Rothbaum & Weisz, 1994), we expected stronger effects of negative parenting for mothers than for fathers. We also hypothesized that (H3) these relations would be moderated by children's gender such that the effects would be stronger for boys than for girls.

METHOD

Participants

Participants in this study were parents of elementary schoolchildren. Part of the sample was recruited randomly with the help of the registry office of a large German city, and another part of the sample was recruited from elementary schools in one district in the vicinity of this city. The two samples did not differ in their main demographic characteristics and were thus collapsed into one. At the first time point, 373 parents (188 mothers and 185 fathers) filled out questionnaires; at the second time point, 326 parents (162 mothers and 164 fathers) responded (response rate: 87%). No selective drop-out was found on demographics, parenting and depressive symptoms except for slightly higher values of depressive symptoms for drop-out fathers, $t(172) = 2.99; p < .05$). Seven cases had to be excluded from the current analyses because of missing data on the relevant scales. The final sample included 319 parents (153 families in which both parents replied; 13 in which only one parent replied; 158 mothers, 161 fathers) who had outcome data at both time points. The mean age of the mothers was 39.4 years ($SD = 3.56$); for the fathers, it was 41.0 years ($SD = 4.0$). Both parents reported on one child in their family in the respective age range (179 boys with a mean age at Time 1 of $M_{boys} = 7.7$ years, $SD = .9$, range: 6–9 years; 140 girls with a mean age at Time 1 of $M_{girls} = 7.3$ years, $SD = 1.0$, range: 5–9 years). The families were primarily intact (99% had been living with their partners for a duration of $M = 13.2$ years; $SD = 4.1$) and of rather high educational background (mothers/fathers: 62.0%/39.8% high school diploma; 38.0%/60.2% some college degree). Participants agreed to complete a self-report questionnaire at both Time 1 and Time 2 (six months later). All couples received €20 for their participation in the study.

Measures

Depressive symptoms were measured at Time 1 with the Simplified Beck Depression Inventory (BDI-V; Schmitt & Maes, 2000), a German short version of the Beck Depression Inventory (Beck & Steer, 1987). The scale consists of 20 items that are rated on a six-point Likert scale from $0 = never$ to $5 = almost$ $always$. Cronbach's αs were $\alpha_{fathers} = .86$ and $\alpha_{mothers} = .89$ (for norms, see Schmitt, Altstötter-Gleich, Hinz, Maes, & Braehler, 2006).

Parenting behaviour was operationalized by positive parenting behaviour and inconsistent discipline, measured at Time 1 and Time 2 with two scales from the German extended version of the Alabama Parenting Questionnaire for Elementary School Age Children (GEAPQ-P-ES; Reichle & Franiek, 2009). The subscales *positive parenting behaviour* and *inconsistent discipline* consist of six items each and are rated on a five-point Likert scale from $1 = hardly$ $ever$ to $= 5$ $almost$ $always$. Cronbach's αs for positive parenting behaviour were $\alpha_{fathers} = .81$ and $\alpha_{mothers} = .79$; for inconsistent discipline: $\alpha_{fathers} = .75$ and $\alpha_{mothers} = .71$).

Children's adjustment was operationalized by oppositional-defiant behaviour, hyperactivity, emotional problems (internalizing) and social-emotional competence. These were measured at Time 2 with the four corresponding scales from the German checklist for behaviour problems and behaviour disorders in preschool-age children (VBV-EL 3-6; Berner, Fleischmann, & Döpfner, 1992; with norms for children from 3;0–7;11 years). The subscales were rated on five-point Likert scales from $0 = never$ or $hardly$ $ever$ to $4 = almost$ $always$. The subscale oppositional-defiant behaviour consists of 10 items with Cronbach's $\alpha_{fathers} = .79$ and $\alpha_{mothers} = .84$, the subscale hyperactivity consists of seven items with Cronbach's $\alpha_{fathers} = .76$ and $\alpha_{mothers} = .77$, the subscale emotional problems/internalizing consists of eight items with Cronbach's $\alpha_{fathers} = .67$ and $\alpha_{mothers} = .68$, and the subscale social-emotional competence consists of nine items with Cronbach's $\alpha_{fathers} = .79$ and $\alpha_{mothers} = .83$.

RESULTS

Preliminary analyses

Descriptive statistics of all scales are shown in Table 1. Depression showed reasonable variability with 82% of the sample in the nonclinical range (individuals with values of 1.75 or higher have a 90% chance of being diagnosed with depression; see Schmitt et al., 2006). Mothers reported higher depression scores and also more positive parenting than fathers. The remaining scales showed no gender differences. Boys scored higher than girls on oppositional-defiant behaviour, $M_{boys} = 1.25$, $M_{girls} = 1.10$, $t(317) = 2.50$, $p < .05$; hyperactivity, $M_{boys} = 1.14$, $M_{girls} = 0.97$, $t(317) = 2.88$, $p < .01$; and lower on socio-emotional competence, $M_{boys} = 2.47$, $M_{girls} = 2.60$, $t(317) = 2.30$, $p < .05$. There was no difference in emotional problems, $M_{boys} = 1.15$, $M_{girls} = 1.12$, $t(317) = 0.51$, ns.

Longitudinal intercorrelations of all study variables were in the expected directions for both mothers and fathers and are shown in Table 2. Depressive symptoms of both parents at Time 1 were positively correlated with children's

TABLE 1
Descriptive statistics of all scales

Scale		n	M	SD	Range	t test
	Time 1					
Depressive symptoms	Mothers	158	1.29	.60	0.1–3.3	$t(317) = 3.36$;
	Fathers	161	1.08	.51	0.1–2.4	$p < .001$
Positive parenting behaviour	Mothers	158	4.37	.47	2.5–5.0	$t(317) = 4.43$;
	Fathers	161	4.13	.50	2.3–5.0	$p < .001$
Inconsistent discipline	Mothers	158	2.45	.56	1.0–4.3	$t(317) = 0.79$;
	Fathers	161	2.49	.52	1.0–4.5	ns
	Time 2					
Oppositional-defiant behaviour	Mothers	158	1.16	.58	0–3.6	$t(317) = 0.96$;
	Fathers	161	1.21	.50	0.2–2.6	ns
Hyperactivity	Mothers	158	1.05	.54	0.1–3.1	$t(317) = 0.70$;
	Fathers	161	1.09	.50	0.1–2.6	ns
Emotional problems/internalizing	Mothers	158	1.09	.49	0.1–2.6	$t(317) = 1.63$;
	Fathers	161	1.18	.48	0–2.6	ns
Social-emotional competence	Mothers	158	2.58	.52	1.2–3.7	$t(317) = 1.95$;
	Fathers	161	2.47	.49	0.7–3.6	ns

oppositional-defiant behaviour, hyperactivity and emotional problems/internalizing and negatively correlated with social-emotional competence at Time 2.

Mothers' and fathers' use of inconsistent discipline was significantly correlated with all child outcome variables. Their positive parenting behaviour was negatively correlated with oppositional-defiant behaviour and positively correlated with social-emotional competence. Fathers' positive parenting was also negatively correlated with hyperactivity.

TABLE 2
Intercorrelations and internal consistencies (Cronbach's αs) for study variables

Variable	1	2	3	4	5	6	7
Predictor variable							
1 Depressive symptoms	*.89/.86*	− .04	.41***	.30***	.19**	.24**	− .23**
Mediators							
2 Positive parenting behaviour	− .17*	*.79/.81*	− .21**	− .17*	− .03	− .08	.28***
3 Inconsistent discipline	.39***	− .13	*.75/.71*	.44***	.40***	.31***	− .34***
Outcome variables							
4 Oppositional-defiant behaviour	.18**	− .14*	.23**	*.84/.79*	.40***	.36***	− .44***
5 Hyperactivity	.14*	− .23**	.18*	.24***	*.77/.76*	.42***	− .38***
6 Emotional problems/internalizing	.27***	− .03	.19**	.38**	.35***	*.68/.67*	− .23**
7 Social-emotional competence	− .18**	.23**	− .24***	− .39***	− .38***	− .13*	*.83/.79*

Notes: Values above the diagonal are for mothers, below are for fathers. Cronbach's α shown in the diagonal (mothers/fathers). $n_{(mothers)} = 158$; $n_{(fathers)} = 161$.
* $p < .05$. ** $p < .01$. *** $p < .001$ (one sided).

Fathers' depressive symptoms were positively correlated with fathers' use of inconsistent discipline and negatively correlated with fathers' positive parenting behaviour, but the two parenting styles positive parenting and inconsistent discipline were uncorrelated. For mothers, however, these were negatively correlated. Also, mothers' depressive symptoms were positively correlated with mothers' use of inconsistent discipline only and unrelated to mothers' positive parenting behaviour.

Model tests

Because of these gender differences in the bivariate correlations and because data of fathers and mothers were dependent, two models were specified in the SPSS module AMOS 19.0. One model tested the effect of fathers' depressive symptoms and parenting on their children's adjustment and the other model tested the effect of mothers' depressive symptoms and parenting on their children's adjustment. According to the hypotheses, paths were assumed between depressive symptoms and parenting and between parenting and children's adjustment, and bivariate correlations were allowed between the different measures of children's adjustment. Because the path between positive parenting and emotional problems/internalizing was nonsignificant for both mothers and fathers and the path between positive parenting and hyperactivity was nonsignificant for mothers, the paths were specified as zero in the respective models. Because we assumed that depressive symptoms would have an immediate effect on parenting (no time lag) and parenting would have a lagged effect on children's adjustment, we chose to model the data with parenting measured at Time 1. Both models yielded a good fit (see Figures 1 and 2).

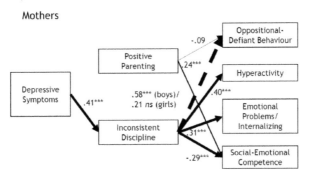

Figure 1. Mediation path model for mothers of the relation between depressive symptoms, parenting and children's adjustment (standardized estimates). $N = 158$; $\chi^2(7) = 7.49$; $p = .38$; Cmin/df = 1.070; TLI = .99; CFI = .997; RMSEA = .021. In bold: complete mediation, dashed: moderated mediation (bootstrap tests with 95% CI, 1000 samples). 95% CIs: Opp-Def Behav: .0709/.2537; Hyp: .0718/.2547; Emot: .0384/.1625; Social: − .1821/− .0470. $^*p < .05.$ $^{**}p < .01.$ $^{***}p < .001.$

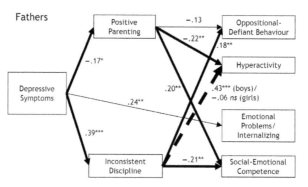

Figure 2. Mediation path model for fathers of the relation between depressive symptoms, parenting and children's adjustment (standardized estimates). $N = 161$; $\chi^2(5) = 3.56$; $p = .614$; Cmin/df $= 0.71$; TLI $= 1.00$; CFI $= 1.00$; RMSEA $= .00$. In bold: complete mediation, dashed: moderated mediation (bootstrap tests with 95% CI, 1000 samples). 95% CIs: Depr via Positive Parenting: Hyp: .0036/.0994; Social: $-$.0838/$-$.0020; Depr via Inc Disc: Opp-Def Behav: .0082/.1576; Hyp: $-$.0286/.1368; Emot: $-$.0402/.1057; Social: $-$.1639/$-$.0232. $^*p < .05$. $^{**}p < .01$. $^{***}p < .001$.

In the next step, all mediated paths were tested for significance using bootstrap tests (SPSS Macro INDIRECT; Preacher & Hayes, 2008; see Figures 1 and 2). In the model for mothers, the bivariate links between mothers' depressive symptoms and all four child adjustment scores were completely mediated by mothers' use of inconsistent discipline. The test for mothers' positive parenting behaviour did not yield any significant results as was expected from the nonsignificant bivariate correlations.

In the model for fathers, the bivariate link between fathers' depressive symptoms and children's oppositional-defiant behaviour was completely mediated by the fathers' use of inconsistent discipline. The bivariate link between fathers' depressive symptoms and children's hyperactivity was completely mediated by fathers' positive parenting behaviour. The bivariate link between fathers' depressive symptoms and children's social competence was completely mediated by both fathers' use of inconsistent discipline and fathers' positive parenting behaviour. The bivariate link between fathers' depressive symptoms and children's emotional problems/internalizing was not mediated by fathers' positive parenting behaviour or fathers' use of inconsistent discipline.

Moderated mediation

In addition to the tests of parent gender differences in the mediation models, gender of the child was analyzed as a potential moderator of the mediation (see Preacher, Rucker, & Hayes, 2007, for the theoretical basis of a moderated mediation model). The tests were performed with the SPSS macro MODMED (Hayes, 2011), which uses a bootstrapping routine. We used 1000 bootstrapped samples and a 95% confidence interval. Of the nine mediated paths tested, two were significant. The link between mothers' use of inconsistent discipline and children's oppositional-defiant behaviour was significant only for boys, but not for girls (see Figure 1; interaction $p = .013$; boys: $\beta = .58$; 95% CI: .391 to .763; girls: $\beta = .21$; 95% CI: $-.003$ to .430). The link between fathers' use of inconsistent discipline and children's hyperactivity was significant only for boys but not for girls (see Figure 2; interaction, $p = .0014$; boys: $\beta = .43$; 95% CI: .215 to .653; girls: $\beta = -.06$; 95% CI: $-.260$ to .146).

DISCUSSION

Parental depressive symptoms have often been shown to have a negative effect on children's adjustment. The present study analyzed longitudinal dyadic data to answer the questions of whether that link would be mediated by parenting, whether there would be gender differences for the parents, and whether the gender of the child would moderate that mediation.

The analyses showed that the bivariate link between parental depressive symptoms and children's adjustment was mediated by parenting style over time. However, the models differed for fathers and mothers. For mothers, only inconsistent parenting behaviour was a mediator of the link between depressive symptoms and children's adjustment. Mothers with less consistent parenting had children with more oppositional defiant behaviour, more hyperactivity, more emotional problems/internalizing and less social-emotional competence. Positive maternal parenting, however, did not act as a mediator. In fact, maternal depressive symptoms and positive parenting style were unrelated over time. A possible reason for this absent relation could be that there were only a few mothers with clinically relevant depressive symptoms in our sample. Many mothers reported only occasional depressive symptoms, and these might not have been intense enough to reduce the positive parenting for these mothers. The occasional depressive symptoms, however, do seem to be influential enough to increase inconsistent parenting for these mothers. In other words, occasional depressive symptoms in mothers seem to lead to occasional periods of lax parenting, which are unpredictable and thus problematic for the children.

For fathers, both positive and inconsistent parenting mediated the relation between paternal depressive symptoms and children's hyperactivity and social-emotional competence. Inconsistent parenting also mediated the relation between paternal depressive symptoms and oppositional-defiant child behaviour. For fathers, it seems that both their consistency and their positivity in child rearing are decreased by occasional depressive symptoms.

For fathers, unlike the mothers, no mediation was found for the relation between depressive symptoms and children's emotional problems/internalizing. Fathers' emotional symptoms provide a model for the children which results in their presentation of emotional symptoms, whereas this was not the case for mothers. Also, the gender of the child did not moderate this relation; thus, the relation between paternal depressive symptoms and children's adjustment was the same for boys and girls.

This missing mediation of the relation between depression and children's emotional problems/internalizing in fathers is not a matter of different associations between depression and parenting: the correlations between depression and inconsistency were almost identical for mothers and fathers, and mothers and fathers with greater levels of depression were equally more inconsistent in their parenting. The extent of inconsistency in mothers and fathers did not differ in a significant way either. But the correlation between parental inconsistency and children's emotional problems/internalizing was much lower for fathers. This means that paternal inconsistency is not threatening for children, but maternal inconsistency is.

This missing relation between paternal inconsistency and children's internalizing might result from fathers usually taking less responsibility for the education of their children, a trend that falls in line with traditional gender roles. As a consequence, inconsistent behaviour by the parent who is perceived as less responsible for the education of children might not be a threat for children, but inconsistent behaviour by the person who is in charge (i.e., the mother) might be. Hence, the weaker relations between fathers' parenting and children's symptoms might be explained by a traditional distribution of responsibilities.

The responsibility of being in charge of the education of one's children might also explain the missing correlation between depression and positive parenting in mothers: a stronger feeling of responsibility for the education of the children might help mothers continue to exhibit positive parenting even if they are depressed. This idea should be tested in further research.

Two of the mediation paths were moderated by children's gender. Mothers' inconsistent parenting and children's oppositional-defiant behaviour and fathers' inconsistent parenting and children's hyperactivity were related only for boys but not for girls. Other studies have also reported similar findings with higher mean scores for boys' externalizing problem behaviour (Cummings et al., 2008; Elgar et al., 2007). In our study, boys also scored higher than girls on oppositional-defiant behaviour and hyperactivity. So, one explanation for the effect on boys but not girls could be the greater necessity for parents to attend to the boys' problem behaviours and also the greater vulnerability of boys to cross the border to disorder if the parenting is not reliable and consistent. These moderated mediation effects need to be looked at closer in further studies.

In general, the results of our study are consistent with several results of previous studies (Amato & Fowler, 2002; Elgar et al., 2007; Rothbaum & Weisz, 1994). The use of dyadic data and dyadic data-analytic techniques lead to a refined picture of the relation between depressive symptoms, parenting and children's adjustment. Unique to this study was that we found gender differences for parents as well as for children. In the bivariate correlations, mothers' but not fathers' positive parenting and inconsistent discipline were negatively correlated. This means that fathers' parenting can be positive no matter how consistent or inconsistent they are, whereas mothers' parenting tends to be less positive the more inconsistent they are. Both mothers and fathers will be less consistent the more depressed they are, but only fathers will also exhibit less positive parenting. Mothers' depressive symptoms were unrelated to mothers' positive parenting. Therefore, mothers with more depressive symptoms will be less consistent, but their parenting will be as positive as the parenting of mothers with fewer depressive symptoms. And even though an increase in positive parenting is very desirable for mothers, our data suggest that depressive symptoms remain a significant predictor of children's adjustment. For mothers, the key to successful parenting despite depressive symptoms seems to be the reduction of inconsistent parenting. The longitudinal link between maternal depressive symptoms and children's adjustment is completely mediated by inconsistent parenting. For fathers, inconsistent parenting also mediates the link between depressive symptoms and children's adjustment, but positive parenting does too for hyperactivity and socio-emotional competence, and there is an additional direct effect of depressive symptoms on children's externalizing behaviour.

In contrast to what we expected from the few previous findings available, there were more effects of fathers' depression than of mothers'. This was primarily due to the additional correlation between (lower) positive paternal parenting and fathers' depression. As expected, boys turned out to be more vulnerable to parental depression and impaired parenting than girls. Like the girls, they showed increased internalizing and were affected in their social-emotional competence independently of the gender of the depressed parent. But in addition, boys of depressed mothers reacted to their mother's heightened inconsistent discipline with increased oppositional-defiant behaviour, and boys of depressed fathers reacted to their father's heightened inconsistent discipline with increased hyperactivity. One might speculate about whether the inconsistent parenting of depressed mothers decreases the status and authority that is ascribed to them by their preadolescent sons, who challenge them with oppositional-defiant behaviour. On the other hand, depressed fathers may be in less danger of losing their status and authority as the inconsistency of depressed fathers is associated with later hyperactivity in boys, a behaviour that is less of a challenge to the status and authority of the parent.

Limitations

Some limitations of the present study need to be mentioned. All measures were taken from the parents because these elementary schoolchildren were too young to provide an accurate account of their problem behaviour. This may have led to inflated relations due to shared variance coming from the same data source. Ideally, this study should be replicated with older children and different sources of data. Also, data were assessed with one method only (questionnaire self-report), which also may have led to inflated relations. Subsequent studies should take other measures into consideration. Moreover, the analyzed models were path models, and thus, all variables were affected by measurement error. Measurement error usually acts to reduce effect sizes and the effects would be estimated more correctly if measurement error was controlled. Although the sample of families was selected randomly, the self-selection involved in answering the questionnaires led to a sample with an overrepresentation of native-speaking educated middle-class families. Less educated and immigrant families were underrepresented, which limits these results to native-speaking middle-class families. Finally, it would be most desirable to replicate the findings using growth curve models that span several years because those models are better able to account for the complexity in developmental processes over time.

CONCLUSION

The implication from these results for practitioners working with families at risk is: strengthening the consistency of parenting behaviours of mothers and fathers is a fruitful approach in general, and it may even be indicated more when parents suffer from depressive symptoms. This may help the children to grow up healthier by weakening the link between their parents' depressive symptoms and parenting style by showing parents how to enact good parenting despite any symptoms of depression that may occur.

REFERENCES

Amato, P. R., & Fowler, F. (2002). Parenting practices, child adjustment, and family diversity. *Journal of Marriage and the Family, 64*, 703–716.

Baumrind, D. (1993). The average expectable environment is not good enough: A response to Scarr. *Child Development, 64*, 1299–1317.

Beck, A. T., & Steer, R. A. (1987). *Beck depression inventory – Manual*. San Antonio, TX: The Psychological Association.

Beelmann, A., Stemmler, M., Lösel, F., & Jaursch, S. (2007). Zur Entwicklung externalisierender Verhaltensprobleme im Übergang vom Vor- zum Grundschulalter: Risikoeffekte des mütterlichen und väterlichen Erziehungsverhaltens [The development of externalizing behaviour problems in the transition from pre- to elementary school age: Risk effects of maternal and paternal parenting]. *Kindheit und Entwicklung, 16*, 229–239.

Berner, W., Fleischmann, T., & Döpfner, M. (1992). Konstruktion von Kurzformen des Eltern- und Erzieherfragebogens zur Erfassung von Verhaltensauffälligkeiten bei Kindern im Vorschulalter [Construction of short forms of the questionnaire for assessing behaviour disturbances in preschoolers]. *Diagnostica, 38*, 142–154.

Blandon, A. Y., Calkins, S. D., Keane, S. P., & O'Brien, M. (2008). Individual differences in trajectories of emotion regulation processes: The effects of maternal depressive symptomatology and children's physiological regulation. *Developmental Psychology, 44*, 1110–1123.

Burt, K. B., van Dulmen, M. H. M., Carlivati, J., Egeland, B., Sroufe, L. A., Forman, D. R., …, Carlson, E. A. (2005). Mediating links between maternal depression and offspring psychopathology: The importance of independent data. *Journal of Child Psychology and Psychiatry, 46*, 490–499.

Conger, R. D., Patterson, G. R., & Ge, X. (1995). It takes two to replicate: A mediational model for the impact of parents' stress on adolescent adjustment. *Child Development, 66*, 80–97.

Cummings, E. M., Schermerhorn, A. C., Keller, P. S., & Davies, P. T. (2008). Parental depressive symptoms, children's representations of family relationships, and child adjustment. *Social Development, 17*, 278–305.

Cummings, E., & Davies, P. T. (1994). Maternal depression and child development. *Journal of Child Psychology and Psychiatry, 35*, 73–112.

Elgar, F. J., Mills, R. L., McGrath, P. J., Waschbusch, D. A., & Brownridge, D. A. (2007). Maternal and paternal depressive symptoms and child maladjustment: The mediating role of parental behavior. *Journal of Abnormal Child Psychology, 35*, 943–955.

Goodman, S. H., & Gotlib, I. H. (1999). Risk for psychopathology in the children of depressed mothers: A developmental model for understanding mechanisms of transmission. *Psychological Review, 106*, 458–490.

Hayes, A. F. (2011). *MODMED* [Program macro]. http://www.afhayes.com/spss-sas-and-mplus-macros-and-code.html

Herwig, J. E., Wirtz, M., & Bengel, J. (2004). Depression, partnership, social support, and parenting: Interaction of maternal factors with behavioral problems of the child. *Journal of Affective Disorders, 80*, 199–208.

Kane, P., & Garber, J. (2004). The relations among depression in fathers, children's psychopathology, and father-child conflict: A meta-analysis. *Clinical Psychology Review, 24*, 339–360.

Karazsia, B. T., & Wildman, B. G. (2009). The mediating effects of parenting behaviors on maternal affect and reports of children's behavior. *Journal of Child and Family Studies, 18*, 342–349.

Koglin, U., & Petermann, F. (2008). Inkonsistentes Erziehungsverhalten: Ein Risikofaktor für aggressives Verhalten? [Inconsistent parental discipline: A risk factor for aggressive behavior?]. *Zeitschrift für Psychiatrie, Psychologie und Psychotherapie, 56*, 285–291.

Kouros, C. D., & Garber, J. (2010). Dynamic associations between maternal depressive symptoms and adolescents' depressive and externalizing symptoms. *Journal of Abnormal Child Psychology, 38*, 1069–1081.

Laible, D. J., & Carlo, G. (2004). The differential relations of maternal and paternal support and control to adolescent social competence, self-worth, and sympathy. *Journal of Adolescent Research, 19*, 759–782.

Laucht, M., Esser, G., & Schmidt, M. H. (2002). Heterogene Entwicklung von Kindern postpartal depressiver Mütter [Heterogeneous development of children of postnatally depressed mothers]. *Zeitschrift für Klinische Psychologie und Psychotherapie: Forschung Und Praxis, 31*, 127–134.

Letourneau, N., Salmani, M., & Duffett-Leger, L. (2010). Maternal depressive symptoms and parenting of children from birth to 12 years. *Western Journal of Nursing Research, 32*, 662–685.

Lovejoy, M., Graczyk, P. A., O'Hare, E., & Neuman, G. (2000). Maternal depression and parenting behavior: A meta-analytic review. *Clinical Psychology Review, 20*, 561–592.

Parent, J., Garai, E., Forehand, R., Roland, E., Potts, J., Haker, K., …, Compas, B. E. (2010). Parent mindfulness and child outcome: The roles of parent depressive symptoms and parenting. *Mindfulness, 1*, 254–264.

Preacher, K. J., & Hayes, A. F. (2008). Asymptotic and resampling strategies for assessing and comparing indirect effects in multiple mediator models. *Behavior Research Methods, 40*, 879–891.

Preacher, K. J., Rucker, D. D., & Hayes, A. F. (2007). Assessing moderated mediation hypotheses: Theory, methods, and prescriptions. *Multivariate Behavioral Research, 42*, 185–227.

Reichle, B., & Franiek, S. (2009). Erziehungsstil aus Elternsicht – Deutsche erweiterte Version des Alabama Parenting Questionnaire für Grundschulkinder [Self-reported parenting style – German extended version of the Alabama Parenting Questionnaire for Elementary School Age Children

(GEAPQ-P-ES)]. *Zeitschrift für Entwicklungspsychologie und Pädagogische Psychologie, 41,* 12–25.

Rothbaum, F., & Weisz, J. R. (1994). Parental caregiving and child externalizing behavior in nonclinical samples: A meta-analysis. *Psychological Bulletin, 116,* 55–74.

Schmitt, M., Altstötter-Gleich, C., Hinz, A., Maes, J., & Braehler, E. (2006). Normwerte für das Vereinfachte Beck-Depressions-Inventar (BDI-V) in der Allgemeinbevölkerung [Norms for the simplified Beck Depression Inventory (BDI-V) in a non-clinical population]. *Diagnostica, 52,* 51–59.

Schmitt, M., & Maes, J. (2000). Vorschlag zur Vereinfachung des Beck-Depressions-Inventars [BDI; Simplification of the Beck Depression Inventory; BDI]. *Diagnostica, 46,* 38–46.

SPSS Amos (19.0) [Computer software]. http://www-03.ibm.com/software/products/gb/en/spss-amos/

Waylen, A., & Stewart-Brown, S. (2010). Factors influencing parenting in early childhood: A prospective longitudinal study focusing on change. *Child: Care, Health & Development, 36,* 198–207.

Wilson, S., & Durbin, C. (2010). Effects of paternal depression on fathers' parenting behaviors: A meta-analytic review. *Clinical Psychology Review, 30,* 167–180.

Gender-specific macro- and micro-level processes in the transmission of gender role orientation in adolescence: The role of fathers

Markus Hess[1], Angela Ittel[2], and Aiden Sisler[2]

[1]Department of Education and Psychology, Freie Universität Berlin, Berlin, Germany
[2]Institute of Education, Technische Universität Berlin, Berlin, Germany

Family represents a primary environment for the development and transmission of gender role orientation (GRO) in adolescence. Nonetheless, longitudinal approaches delineating the separate influences of fathers and mothers, including all possible same- and cross-sex parent–child dyads within one family are lacking. This article elucidates the process of adolescent gender role socialization in 244 German families (father, mother, son and daughter) utilizing a longitudinal design (two measurement points over 5 years). Direct transmission paths of GRO and gender-specific parenting (GSP) as a mediator were analysed focusing on fathers' contributions. In addition, the impact of parental workplace autonomy and socio-economic status on intra-familial socialization of GRO was examined. Results indicate that fathers and mothers play at least an equally important role in the transmission of gender role beliefs. A mediating effect of GSP was only evident when considering father–child dyads. Based on social cognitive and developmental systems approaches, the findings are discussed considering adolescents embedded within the family context.

Understanding how an individual's gender role orientation (GRO) is formed within a family aids in shedding light on future social adjustment and development (Davis & Greenstein, 2009). In this study, we target GRO which reflects the level

We want to explicitly thank the Deutsche Forschungsgemeinschaft (DFG) for supporting this project as well as our valued colleagues Hans Merkens, Poldi Kuhl, Tina Kretschmer and Susanne Bergann.

of agreement with cultural expectations concerning gender-related behaviour and the distribution of labour between the sexes (Galambos, 2004). Despite the growing influence by peers, teachers and the media (Martin, Wood, & Little, 1990), the family continues to be an important environment in the formation and transmission of GRO during adolescence (Carlson & Knoester, 2011).

Nevertheless, longitudinal studies illuminating the gender-specific influence of mothers and fathers on their adolescent offspring in a within-family design, thus appraising the family as a whole unit, are lacking. This article puts forth a differentiated model of GRO development by considering potential influencing factors based on two ecological levels of family socialization. As most studies have focused on maternal contributions, this study aims to elucidate paternal influence in the process of GRO formation (Davis & Wills, 2010).

Gender role transmission within families

Parents' attitudes and behaviours concerning gender are precursors in children's gender development (Ruble, Martin, & Berenbaum, 2006); GRO of parents and their offspring are often linked (e.g., Tenenbaum & Leaper, 2002). Relating a developmental systems approach highlighting the socio-environmental context and emphasizing the transactional nature of the person-environment interrelation to the transmission of GRO (Lerner, Rothbaum, Boulos, & Castellino, 2002) implies that adolescents' bring in their individual-level attributes to the transmission process and react differentially to parental behaviour (Scheithauer, Niebank, & Ittel, 2009). In addition, from a social cognitive and learning perspective, parental influence may be exerted through modelling processes (Bussey & Bandura, 1999) and direct parenting practices (McHale, Crouter, & Whiteman, 2003). In the present study, modelling processes are reflected by similarities in GRO between parents and their offspring (attitudinal parameter) and parenting practices through adolescents' gender-specific parenting (GSP) experiences (behavioural parameter).

A traditional GRO reflects a gendered orientation towards the distribution of labour, whereby women do housework and provide childcare and men are responsible for providing economic resources. This labour distribution is considered more favourable for men since social reputation is tied to occupational status. Indeed, male privilege and dominance intrinsic to patriarchal systems continue to be reflected in more traditional gender role attitudes by males than by females (Burt & Scott, 2002; Zuo & Tang, 2000). On a societal level, these beliefs are challenged by gender mainstreaming and equality efforts in professional settings, and further reflected in mothers' labour force participation and the growing amount of time fathers devote to childcare (Bianchi & Milkie, 2010).

From a developmental systems perspective, it is tenable that daughters—seen as active agents of their development—will be especially prone to challenging traditional GRO and therefore hold the lowest level of traditional GRO, and sons will exhibit the most traditional GRO in an attempt to maintain their status advantage (Sidanius & Pratto, 2001). In accordance with gender intensification theory, which holds that the tendency to adhere to traditional gender roles intensifies in adolescence (Priess, Lindberg, & Hide, 2009), we postulate that boys' traditional GRO will be more exaggerated than girls (e.g., Jackson & Tein, 1998).

Referring to assumptions proposed by the social cognitive theory of gender development (Bussey & Bandura, 1999) and the sex role model (Acock & Bengston, 1978), we hypothesize that parental GRO is reflected in parents' behaviour observed by their children. In addition, when both parents are present, children tend to use the same-sex parent as the focal model (Bussey & Bandura, 1999). Therefore, we speculate that same-sex intergenerational similarities in GRO are greater than cross-sex similarities.

Parents' differential treatment of boys and girls when rewarding behaviour assists in shaping children's gendered behaviour and attitudes (Mischel & Liebert, 1966). This gender-specific parenting (GSP) is believed to reflect parents' underpinning GRO. While egalitarian mothers tend to have less traditional gender-role stereotyped offspring (Myers & Booth, 2002), the relative impact of parental modeling, practices and gendered ideology is difficult to disentangle (Davis & Wills, 2010). Studies on GSP have found that parents more often foster independence in boys, whereas girls are raised to be dependent (Leaper & Friedman, 2007). Previous literature equivocates, however, on the degree to which gender differences operate in other parent–child interactions considering the whole family system (e.g., Lytton & Romney, 1991). Disparities were cited in the reinforcement of gender-typed activities but were absent in other realms. Moreover, fathers were instrumental in gender socialization with sons in particular, although, again, between-family findings could not account for interactive value transmission (Lytton & Romney, 1991).

One conceptual and methodological shortcoming in addressing intra-familial transmission of GRO regards the confounding of between and within effects. Only the comparison of fathers, mothers and offspring of different sexes simultaneously within one family allows for reliable gender-specific intra-familial analyses (McHale et al., 2003). In order to illuminate gender-specific processes in transmission and possible sex variances in GRO similarities, we incorporated different micro- (parenting style and GRO congruence) and macro-level (parental workplace) factors into our within family analysis.

Micro-level factors in GRO transmission

Ecological theory (Bronfenbrenner, 1979) privileges multiple interacting systems regarding influences on the nested individuals' attitudes and behaviour. Within the most proximal micro-system, an individual's daily life setting (home), roles, relationships and daily activities are deemed to be critical elements in gender development (Stevenson, 1991). A number of studies detected significant correlations in the mother–daughter relationship concerning measures of attitudes regarding the role of females in society, GRO and over-arching gender role beliefs (e.g., Ex & Janssens, 1998). These findings were interpreted such that same sex homogeneity was particularly salient in the transmission of GRO between parents and children as predicted by social learning theory (Bussey & Bandura, 1999).

A more complex picture emerges when appraising the few studies which included parent–child dyads other than mother–daughter pairs. Thornton, Alwin, and Camburn (1983) found similar associations of GRO between mothers and children of both sexes over time. Other cross-sectional studies have found significant correlations in all possible dyads even detecting a stronger father–child than mother–child GRO link (Kulik, 2002; O'Bryan, Fishbein, & Ritchey, 2004). Burt and Scott (2002) further concluded that same-sex associations of GRO are generally not stronger than cross-sex associations. A meta-analysis conducted by Fishbein (2002) highlighted the significant role of mothers and the important—albeit often neglected—contribution of fathers in inter-generational transmission.

Targeting a unique sample through the use of an apposite whole family design, the present research addresses two questions at the micro-level concerning the role of GSP. First, we investigate whether sons and daughters experience differential parenting within a family system and, additionally, if GSP mediates the direct relation between parent and offspring GRO concordance rates considering select macro-level variables.

Macro-level factors in GRO transmission

Macro-level factors reflect processes that stem from extra-familial contexts, such as workplace conditions and social economic status (Bianchi & Milkie, 2010). With regard to power-control theory developed by Hagan, Simpson, and Gillis (1987), we hypothesize that working conditions, namely the degree of parental workplace autonomy (WPA), rather than occupation itself contribute to the interfamilial transmission of GRO. In families where fathers hold autonomous and dominant positions at the workplace, traditional gender roles and GSP will be maintained, whereas in families where mothers experience autonomous workplace conditions traditional GRO will likely be challenged (Cleveland, Stockdale, Murphy, & Gutek, 2000).

Earlier studies offer evidence that higher levels of parental education and income correspond to more egalitarian attitudes regarding gender role attitudes (e.g., Kulik, 2002). We therefore expected that high familial socio-economic status (SES) [combining educational level and family income, Mueller and Parcel (1981)] corresponds with low overall adherence to traditional GRO.

It is worth bearing in mind that the directionality of socio-contextual factors and the individual-level factor of gender ideology is as of yet inconclusive; those individuals with egalitarian GRO may be more likely to occupy positions in egalitarian environments which may then interact in a mutually supportive process. Evidence pointing in this direction was provided by Sidanius and Pratto (2001) with the related construct of social dominance orientation. We do not speculate at length regarding the directionality of GRO and occupational choice gleaned from longitudinal analyses as it is outside the scope of this report, although we do acknowledge its future importance.

Figure 1 provides a graphical summary of the hypotheses of the present study. On the macro-level, it is expected that high SES is associated with more egalitarian parental GRO. It is assumed that fathers' high WPA corresponds with more traditional GRO particularly when mothers' WPA is low. Mothers' high WPA is believed to correspond with more egalitarian GRO independent of fathers' degree of WPA. On the micro-level, GSP is expected to mediate the relation between parental and offspring GRO. Moreover, parental GRO is proposed to be transmitted to adolescent children in a direct manner, with same-sex transmission paths expected to be stronger than cross-sex paths.

METHOD

Sample

Data stem from a longitudinal questionnaire study conducted in Berlin, Germany with two measurement points (1999, 2004). Only families consisting of a father, a

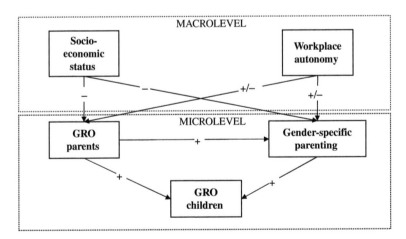

Figure 1. Research model describing potential influences on the parent–child transmission of traditional GRO. *Notes:* A plus sign indicates an enhancing influence and a minus sign a reducing effect. The combined plus and minus signs divided by a slash reflect gender-specific assumptions concerning the influence of workplace authority (minus signs hold for mothers and plus signs hold for fathers). GRO, traditional gender role orientation.

mother[1] and an adolescent son and daughter qualified to participate in order to examine the distinct dyadic gender combinations. At the first measurement point, 504 complete family tetrads were included. Five years later, 244 families were recruited (48.4%). The high dropout rate is likely due to the long time span between measurements (5 years), low direct participant contact due to the postal survey design, and only families who provided full data for all four members were considered for the final sample. Therefore, we consider the drop out as missing at random (Rubin, 1976). Data were only available for the longitudinal sample, so comparison between those who remained in the sample and those who dropped out after time 1 was not possible. The present sample has a mean age of 14.12 years [standard deviation (SD) = 2.40] for sons and 14.37 years (SD = 2.14) for daughters at the first measurement point. Age of parents was not measured in the survey, and 12 children (4.5%) lived with at least one step-parent. As the number of step-parents is rather low in the sample, no further analyses including this variable were conducted. SES was rather homogenous. Parents were generally highly educated with an average of 11.4 years of education for mothers and 11.52 years for fathers; few parents completed less than 10 years of school (2.6% of mothers and 5.8% of fathers). Most fathers (92.0%) and mothers (77.9%) were employed, and 69.3% of the families had no additional children other than the son and the daughter who participated in the study. The remaining families had three to five children with three children for 21.9% of families, four children for 4.2% and five children for 3.1% of families.

Procedure

Data were gathered from 58 schools in Berlin, Germany. A preliminary screening was conducted to select grade 7–10 adolescents who fulfilled the participatory requirements (i.e., living with both parents and with one opposite-sex adolescent sibling in the same household). Following active parental consent for participation in the study of the selected adolescents, trained researchers administered the standardised questionnaire to the children. Parents and siblings were asked to send their questionnaire in a pre-stamped envelope. For the secondary data collection, families were once again contacted through the participating adolescent at school or—when participants had left the school—via mail. A lottery for minor incentives was held among the participants.

---

[1]In order to be allowed to participate, the father and mother had to live with the participating adolescents but were not required to be a biological parent.

Measures

Dependent/moderator variables
Traditional GRO. We used four items from a German version of a scale (Krampen, 1983) concerning traditional gender-typed expectations of labour participation and power division. All four family members indicated the extent to which they agreed with statements, such as "Women should enter traditionally masculine professions like brick layer or pilot more often" on a scale from 1 ("strong disagreement") to 5 ("strong agreement"). High mean scores on this scale designate strong agreement to traditional gender roles. Parents' GRO at the first time point and children's GRO at the second time point were included in the analysis. Cronbach's α for this scale indicated sufficient internal consistency for the purpose of the present study ($\alpha_{mothers} = .67$; $\alpha_{fathers} = .74$; $\alpha_{sons} = .81$; $\alpha_{daughters} = .61$).

Independent variables
Microlevel. GSP. At the second time point, a 4-item subscale measuring GSP was included (Hoffman & Kloska, 1995). Items were modified such that children answered questions about their mother's and father's parenting separately. Sample items include "For my mother/father it was more important to raise a son to be strong and independent than to raise a daughter (to be strong and independent)" and "My mother/father saw nothing wrong with giving a boy a doll to play with". Agreement with the statements was measured on a five-point Likert scale. Due to high correlations of ratings provided by one adolescent ($r_{son} = .91$ and $r_{daughter} = .85$, respectively), ratings were summarized into one index of parental GSP per adolescent. Despite Cronbach's α ranged from .53 to .61, we opted to include these scales due to the study's broad operationalization of GSP; GSP represents a heterogeneous construct which often goes along with relatively low reliability ratings (Streiner, 2003).

Macrolevel. WPA. Both parents' WPA was assessed through six questions based on Hagan, Boehnke, and Merkens (2004). Sample items included, "Do you give advice to other co-workers?" or "Do you carry out instructions from other co-workers?" in a dichotomous answer format ($1 = $ "no"; $2 = $ "yes"). After necessary re-coding, a mean sum score was then calculated with high scores indicating high levels of WPA. For the present paper, parental ratings of time 1 are included in the analysis.
SES. Familial SES was measured at time 1 by averaging standardized mothers' and fathers' ratings of educational level (in years) and family income per month (in Euros).

TABLE 1
Study descriptives

Variable	Male participants		Female participants		
	M	SD	M	SD	t
Microlevel					
GRO-C (1–5)	2.08	0.88	1.40	0.49	11.87***
GRO-P (1–5)	1.70	0.75	1.47	0.57	4.58***
GSP (1–5)	1.74	0.30	1.51	0.58	4.80***
Macrolevel					
WPA (0–1)	0.51	0.30	0.38	0.26	5.41***
SES (1–7)	4.59	1.27	4.59	1.27	–

Notes: SES, socio-economic status; GSP, gender-specific parenting; GRO, traditional gender role orientation; WPA, workplace autonomy; C, child; P, parent. ***$p < .001$.

RESULTS

Table 1 provides an overview of relevant descriptive statistics. Male participants (sons and fathers) display higher traditional GRO than their female counterparts. In addition, sons perceive more gender-specific child rearing by their parents than daughters. Fathers indicated higher WPA than mothers.

Bivariate correlations between all study variables were conducted (Table 2) and missing data were replaced with maximum-likelihood estimations. GROs of all family members were positively correlated. In addition, no significant differences concerning the bivariate correlations between the generations or

TABLE 2
Bivariate correlations of the study variables (correlations of the measurement models, maximum-likelihood estimation, $N = 244$)

	01.	02.	03.	04.	05.	06.	07.	08.
Microlevel								
01. GRO-S (2)	–							
02. GRO-D (2)	.41***	–						
03. GRO-F (1)	.54***	.36***	–					
04. GRO-M (1)	.34***	.44***	.41***	–				
05. GSP-S (2)	.75***	.04 ns	.32***	.13 ns	–			
06. GSP-D (2)	.26**	.41***	.38***	.13 ns	.38***	–		
Macrolevel								
07. WPA-F (1)	.06 ns	− .04 ns	.05 ns	.16⁺	.10 ns	.00 ns	–	
08. WPA-M (1)	.00 ns	− .01 ns	.03 ns	.02 ns	− .05 ns	.00 ns	.21**	–
09. SES (1)	− .25**	− .21*	− .16*	− .27**	− .44***	− .26**	.23**	.23**

Notes: GRO, traditional gender role orientation; GSP, gender-specific parenting; FSC, family sense of coherence; SES, socio-economic status; WPA, workplace autonomy; M, mother; F, father; S, son; D, daughter; timepoint in parentheses; ns, not significant. $^{+}p < .10$; *$p < .05$; **$p < .01$; ***$p < .001$.

between the sexes were found (applying Fisher's z-values). In examination of the relation between GROs of parents and the ratings of GSP as experienced by the adolescents, results illustrate that only fathers' GRO was associated with GSP practices for both sons and daughters ($r_{son} = .32$, $p < .001$ and $r_{daughter} = .38$, $p < 001$). For mothers, no significant correlation was detected ($r_{son} = .13$, ns and $r_{daughter} = .13$, ns). We attend to this unexpected finding in the "Discussion" section. Additional variables not depicted in Table 2, such as age of the adolescents and total number of siblings in the family, did not correlate significantly with intra-familiar GRO or parenting practices, therefore they were not considered in further analyses.

No significant relationships between the WPA of mothers and fathers or the micro-level variables were identified. The link between SES, representing another macro-level factor, and the micro-level factors of GRO and GSP confirmed initial expectations. Members of families with a high SES showed more egalitarian GRO and less GSP than members of families with lower SES status.

To test the associations between macro-level and micro-level factors in the transmission of GRO within families on a multivariate level, we conducted several structural equation models (SEM) using AMOS 5. Before running the overall structural models, we separately tested the goodness of fit for the measurement models of GRO and GSP. These analyses revealed sufficient fitting indices for all measurement models with root mean square error of approximation (RMSEA) between .00 and .08 and comparative fit index (CFI) between 1.00 and .97 (Bentler, 1990).

In the initial SEM, similarity between parental GRO at time 1 and their children's GRO at time 2 was examined. As seen in Figure 2, results revealed a strong same-sex connection for father–son and mother–daughter dyad. Moreover, data revealed a significant relation between fathers' and daughters' GRO, whereas the other cross-sex path between mothers and sons was not significant. However, further comparison between a model of cross-sex paths

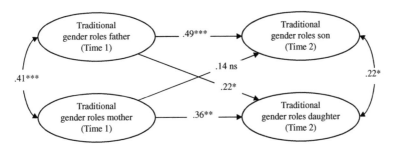

Figure 2. Parent–child transmission across a 4-year period ($\chi^2[98] = 119.77$; CFI $= .98$; RMSEA $= .03$; standardized coefficients, maximum-likelihood-estimation; ns, not significant. $*p < .05$; $**p < .01$, $***p < .001$).

TABLE 3
Results of model comparisons testing for mediation of the parent–child link in GROs through GSP

Model	$\chi^2(df)$	χ^2/df	CFI	RMSEA	$\Delta\chi^2(df)$
Full mediation model	327.55(239)	1.37	.929	.039	
No mediation model	421.18(245)	1.72	.859	.054	93.623(6)***
Only mother mediation	350.29(241)	1.45	.913	.043	22.735(2)***
Only father mediation	327.56(241)	1.36	.931	.038	.001(2) ns

Notes: ns, not significant. ***$p < .001$.

which were constrained to be equal and a model with no restrictions revealed no significant difference ($\chi_\Delta[1] = .41$, $p = .52$). That is, although the significance levels between the cross-sex paths differed, they do not differ substantially.

To test the mediating role of GSP, we compared different nested models with a full model, i.e., initially a model with no parameter restrictions was constructed after which several parameters within this model were restricted based on theoretical assumptions. These restricted models are termed "nested" because they are all based on the unrestricted model. In a second step, we compared χ^2 statistics of these nested models with the unrestricted model (e.g., Frazier, Tix, & Barron, 2004). The present study compared four models. In the full mediation model, none of the model parameters are restricted. In the no-mediation model, we set the paths between the GRO of parents and adolescents and the GSP variable to a value of zero, assuming that there is no effect. This was done for mothers and fathers separately and for both parents simultaneously. If there are no significant differences between the models or if the models that include the forced restrictions reveal a better fit than the unrestricted model, it can be assumed that there is no mediation effect of GSP (see Table 3).

Of the four models, the one with the best fit restricted both paths from mothers' GRO to the ratings of the GSP to a value of zero, and the same paths for the father were left unrestricted ($\chi^2[241] = 327.55$; CFI $= .931$; RMSEA $= .038$). The GRO of mothers did not influence the degree of GSP, whereas a strong link between fathers' GRO and their GSP was detected.

The final mediation model with standardized path coefficients is shown below (see Figure 3). The direct paths between paternal and adolescent GRO are reduced compared to the previous model without mediating variables (father–son from $\beta = .49$ to $\beta = .25$ and father–daughter from $\beta = .22$ to $\beta = .09$). The father–son path remained significant, which might suggest a partial mediation effect of GSP on the transmission of GROs. Second, only paternal GRO had an influence on the rating of the GSP of boys and girls ($\beta_{father/son} = .36$ and $\beta_{father/daughter} = .38$). Furthermore, the ratings of GSP were related to the GRO of adolescent boys and girls, yet this influence was stronger for boys than for girls ($\beta_{son} = .64$ and $\beta_{daughter} = .33$). Additional Sobel-tests (Baron & Kenny, 1986)

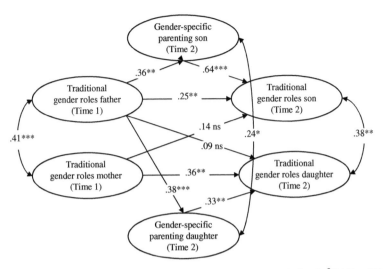

Figure 3. The mediating role of GSP in explaining parent–child transmission ($\chi^2[241] = 327.55$; CFI $= .931$; RMSEA $= .038$; standardized coefficients, maximum-likelihood-estimation; *ns*, not significant. $*p < .05$; $**p < .01$; $***p < .001$).

to check for significant mediation of GSP on GRO transmission in the different parent–child combinations (father/son, father/daughter, mother/son and mother/daughter) confirmed a mediation effect for both father–child dyads ($z_{father/son} = 2.70$, $p < .01$ and $z_{father/daughter} = 2.48$, $p < .05$) but not for the mother–child dyads ($z_{mother/son} = 1.24$, $p = .21$ and $z_{mother/daughter} = 1.40$, $p = .16$).

In a final step, the macro-level variables (i.e., WPA and SES) were incorporated into the model. There were no significant relationships between parental WPA and any of the micro-level variables from the bivariate analyses; WPA was only related to the SES of the families. In addition, due to the results of the preliminary SEM, the paths from mother GRO to the child ratings of GSP were eliminated (see Figure 4). Higher SES corresponded with lower traditional GRO and with lower levels of GSP.

DISCUSSION

Based on the within-family design, the first aim of the present study was to clarify gender differences in parent–child transmission of GRO. As expected from social cognitive theory, our results revealed that same-sex GRO similarities were stronger than cross-sex similarities. Nevertheless, adolescents and girls in particular seem to identify to some degree with their cross-sex parent's gender role beliefs. This confirms previous findings emphasizing the role of fathers in the intra-familiar transmission of gender stereotypes (O'Bryan et al., 2004). Another viable explanation privileging the transactional nature of family systems

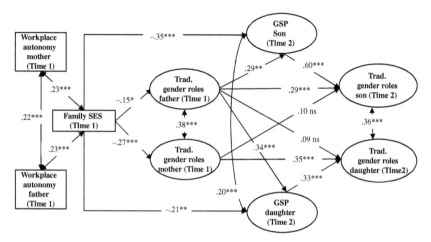

Figure 4. The role of macro-level factors (WPA and SES) on the micro-level processes of parent–child transmission of GRO ($\chi^2[309] = 411.9$, RMSEA $= .04$, CFI $= .93$; standardized coefficients, maximum-likelihood-estimation. $^+p < .10$, $*p < .05$; $**p < .01$, $***p < .001$).

contends that fathers with daughters become more egalitarian over time (Shafer & Malhotra, 2011). Moreover, egalitarian fathers may increasingly influence ideology construction through participation in child rearing, and especially value daughters. Additionally, we found that sons held more traditional GRO than any other family member, corroborating our expectation drawing on gender intensification theory (Priess et al., 2009). That is, within the realm of changing societal norms concerning gendered distribution of labour, boys may hold onto traditional orientations in order to secure their status advantage, whereas daughters challenge traditional gender roles (Scott, Dex, & Joshi, 2008).

The second objective was to depict factors influencing the role of mothers and fathers simultaneously in the transference of gender roles. We found strong similarities in ratings of children concerning the degree of GSP of both parents, yet sons perceive parenting as more gender-specific than daughters. The data depicted a mediating effect of GSP on GRO transmission only in father–child dyads. In the father–son dyad, the direct paths between parental and adolescent GRO remained significant indicating an association of intergenerational GRO transmission above and beyond the influence of GSP; fathers may actively rear their offspring according to their own GRO.

Our results further indicate that maternal GRO, in contrast to paternal GRO, is independent of adolescent ratings of GSP. We propose two mechanisms: first, we speculate that the degree to which the GRO (as a rating of normative aspects of gender roles in society) is internalized into the gendered concept of the self and functions as a guideline for behaviour may vary across gender. That is, fathers may feel more responsible than mothers in the communication of their values (egalitarian or traditional) to their children (O'Bryan et al., 2004). Additional exploratory analysis of the present data revealed that ratings of GRO by fathers were more strongly related to their gender identity (Wilson & Liu, 2003) than ratings provided by mothers. However, these preliminary results require further examination.

A second explication for the missing link between mothers' GRO and their GSP may hinge on mothers' low GSP ratings. Fathers also rated fairly low but nonetheless reared their children in a more gender-specific manner than mothers. It should be noted that GSP SDs were equal for mothers and fathers, eliminating inequality of variance as a potential confound. Mothers likely model an egalitarian GRO within the present sample through their employment such that GSP is not as salient in GRO transmission. In addition, longitudinal studies have found that mothers who contribute to the total family income become more egalitarian (Zuo & Tang, 2000).

SEM revealed that sons are more susceptible to the incorporation of GSP practices into their gender role beliefs than daughters. When viewed from the varied privileges and power distributions that gender-specific socialization instils in sons and daughters, the traditional gendered power division and accompanying GRO benefit males and may then be more readily assimilated by boys. Thus, sons might agree with GSP and to fit these parenting experiences into their individual set of roles, norms and values. In sum, the results of our micro-level analyses highlight the role of the father in the intra-familial transmission of gender roles in adolescence and point to the critical need to consider male family members in questions of gender-specific socialization.

Concerning the influence of macro-level factors in the transmission of gender-roles within families, WPA was not associated with the degree of adherence to a traditional GRO. This result may be due in part to the fact that there was relatively little variance in WPA and SES. Nevertheless we found that higher SES corresponded with more egalitarian GRO. It would be valuable to separate the different aspects of SES in further study to assess which component (education or income) has a stronger influence on GRO.

The present research bears some limitations. Ratings of GSP were assessed only at the last measurement point, so the analysis of the influence of GSP on adolescent GRO remained cross-sectional. To address the issue of social desirability inherent in using attitudinal measures, forthcoming studies should include behaviour-oriented measures, e.g., gender-specific day-to-day activities (McHale, Crouter, & Tucker, 1999). Notably our sample is fairly homogenous, and thus the majority of the variables possessed relatively low levels of variance. On the micro-level, family structure factors such as step-parent status, family climate or parent–child relationship quality should be considered as should differentiated aspects of workplace structure and work–life balance beyond WPA (e.g., time spent with children and at work, separation of parental income or profession gender-typed characteristics).

That notwithstanding, this research offers insights into the processes of GRO transmission beyond the mere similarity in attitudes between parents and children. The results stress the importance of considering the critical role of fathers and gender-specific transmission processes in studies on gender socialization in adolescence. Future inquiry would do well to explore additional variables and their interrelationships to advance understanding of the ideological connections between parents and their daughters and sons in interconnected family systems.

REFERENCES

Acock, A. C., & Bengtson, V. L. (1978). On the relative influence of mothers and fathers: A covariance analysis of political and religious socialisation. *Journal of Marriage and the Family, 40*, 519–530.

Baron, R. M., & Kenny, D. A. (1986). The moderator–mediator variable distinction in social psychological research: Conceptual, strategic, and statistical considerations. *Journal of Personality and Social Psychology, 51*, 1173–1182.

Bentler, P. M. (1990). Comparative fit indexes in structural models. *Psychological Bulletin, 107*, 238–246.

Bianchi, S. M., & Milkie, M. A. (2010). Work and family research in the first decade of the 21st century. *Journal of Marriage and Family, 72*, 705–725.

Bronfenbrenner, U. (1979). *The ecology of human development: Experiments by nature and design.* Cambridge: Harvard University Press.

Burt, K. B., & Scott, J. (2002). Parent and adolescent gender role attitudes in 1990s Great Britain. *Sex Roles, 46*, 239–245.

Bussey, K., & Bandura, A. (1999). Social cognitive theory of gender development and differentiation. *Psychological Review, 106*, 676–713.

Carlson, D. L., & Knoester, C. (2011). Family structure and the intergenerational transmission of gender ideology. *Journal of Family Issues, 32*, 709–734.

Cleveland, J. N., Stockdale, M., Murphy, K. R., & Gutek, B. A. (2000). *Women and men in organizations: Sex and gender issues at work.* Mahwah, NJ: Psychology Press.

Davis, S. N., & Greenstein, T. N. (2009). Gender ideology: Components, predictors, and consequences. *Annual Review of Sociology, 35*, 87–105.

Davis, S. N., & Wills, J. B. (2010). Adolescent gender ideology socialization: Direct and moderating effects of fathers' beliefs. *Sociological Spectrum, 30*, 580–604.

Ex, C. T., & Janssens, J. M. (1998). Maternal influences on daughters' gender role and attitudes. *Sex Roles, 38*, 171–186.

Fishbein, H. D. (2002). *Peer prejudice and discrimination: Origins of prejudice.* Mahwah, NJ: Erlbaum.

Frazier, P. A., Tix, A. P., & Barron, K. E. (2004). Testing moderator and mediator effects in counseling psychology research. *Journal of Counseling Psychology, 51*, 115–134.

Galambos, N. L. (2004). Gender and gender role development in adolescence. In R. M. Lerner & L. Steinberg (Eds.), *Handbook of adolescent psychology* (2nd ed.) (pp. 233–262). New York, NY: Wiley.

Hagan, J., Boehnke, K., & Merkens, H. (2004). Gender differences in capitalization processes and the delinquency of siblings in Toronto and Berlin. *British Journal of Criminology, 44*, 659–676.

Hagan, J., Simpson, J., & Gillis, A. R. (1987). Class in the household: A power-control theory of gender and delinquency. *American Journal of Sociology, 92*, 788–816.

Hoffman, L. W., & Kloska, D. D. (1995). Parents' gender-based attitudes toward marital roles and child rearing: Development and validation of new measures. *Sex Roles, 32*, 273–295.

Jackson, D., & Tein, J. (1998). Adolescents' conceptualization of adult roles: Relationships with age, gender, work goals, and maternal employment. *Sex Roles, 38*, 987–1008.

Krampen, G. (1983). Eine Kurzform der Skala zur Messung normativer Geschlechtsrollen-Orientierungen [A short version of the scale for the measurement of normative gender-role orientations]. *Zeitschrift für Soziologie, 12*, 152–156.

Kulik, L. (2002). Like-sex versus opposite-sex effects in transmission of gender role ideology from parents to adolescents in Israel. *Journal of Youth and Adolescence, 31*, 451–457.

Leaper, C., & Friedman, C. K. (2007). The socialization of gender. In J. Grusec & P. Hastings (Eds.), *Handbook of socialization: Theory and research* (pp. 561–587). New York, NY: Guilford Press.

Lerner, R. M., Rothbaum, F., Boulos, S., & Castellino, D. R. (2002). Developmental systems perspective on parenting. In M. H. Bornstein (Ed.), *Handbook of parenting* (2nd ed.) (pp. 315–344). Mahwah, NJ: Erlbaum.

Lytton, H., & Romney, D. M. (1991). Parents' differential socialization of boys and girls: A meta-analysis. *Psychological Bulletin, 109*, 267–297.

Martin, C. L., Wood, C. H., & Little, J. K. (1990). The development of gender stereotype components. *Child Development, 61*, 1891–1904.

McHale, S. M., Crouter, A. C., & Tucker, C. J. (1999). Family context and gender socialization in middle childhood: Comparing girls to boys and sisters to brothers. *Child Development, 70*, 990–1004.

McHale, S. M., Crouter, A. C., & Whiteman, S. D. (2003). The family contexts of gender development in childhood and adolescence. *Social Development, 12*, 125–148.

Mischel, H. N., & Liebert, R. M. (1966). Effects of discrepancies between observed and imposed reward criteria on their acquisition and transmission. *Journal of Personality and Social Psychology, 2*, 45–53.

Mueller, C. W., & Parcel, T. L. (1981). Measures of socioeconomic status: Alternatives and recommendations. *Child Development, 52*, 13–30.

Myers, S., & Booth, A. (2002). Forerunners of change in nontraditional gender ideology. *Social Psychology Quarterly, 65*, 18–37.

O'Bryan, M., Fishbein, H. D., & Ritchey, P. N. (2004). Intergenerational transmission of prejudice, sex role stereotyping, and intolerance. *Adolescence, 39*, 407–426.

Priess, H. A., Lindberg, S. M., & Hyde, J. S. (2009). Adolescent gender-role identity and mental health: Gender intensification revisited. *Child Development, 80*, 1531–1544.

Rubin, D. B. (1976). Inference and missing data. *Biometrika, 63*, 581–592.

Ruble, D. N., Martin, C. L., & Berenbaum, S. A. (2006). Gender development. In W. Damon, R.M. Lerner (Series Eds.), N. Eisenberg (Vol. Ed.). *Handbook of child psychology: Vol. 3. Social, emotional and personality development* (6th ed., pp. 858–932). Hoboken, NJ: Wiley.

Scheithauer, H., Niebank, K., & Ittel, A. (2009). Developmental science: Integrating knowledge about dynamic processes in human development. In J. Valsiner, P. Molenar, & M. Lyra (Eds.), *Dynamic process methodology in the social and developmental sciences* (pp. 595–617). New York, NY: Springer.

Scott, J., Dex, S., & Joshi, H. (2008). *Women and employment: Changing lives and new challenges.* Cheltenham: Edward Elgar.

Shafer, E. F., & Malhotra, N. (2011). The effect of a child's sex on traditional gender roles: Evidence from a natural experiment. *Social Forces, 90*, 209–222.

Sidanius, J., & Pratto, F. (2001). *Social dominance: An intergroup theory of social hierarchy and oppression.* New York, NY: Cambridge University Press.

Stevenson, M. R. (1991). Perceptions of relationship with father and sex-typed characteristics of offspring. *Sex Roles, 24*, 239–244.

Streiner, D. L. (2003). Starting at the beginning: An introduction to coefficient alpha and internal consistency. *Journal of Personality Assessment, 80*, 99–103.

Tenenbaum, H. R., & Leaper, C. (2002). Are parents' gender schemas related to their children's gender-related cognitions?: A meta analysis. *Developmental Psychology, 38*, 615–630.

Thornton, A., Alwin, D. F., & Camburn, D. (1983). Causes and consequences of sex-role attitudes and attitude change. *American Sociological Review, 43*, 211–227.

Wilson, M. S., & Liu, J. H. (2003). Social dominance orientation and gender: The moderating role of gender identity. *British Journal of Social Psychology, 42*, 187–198.

Zuo, J., & Tang, S. (2000). Breadwinner status and gender ideologies of men and women regarding family roles. *Sociological Perspectives, 43*, 29–43.

Effects of different facets of paternal and maternal control behaviour on early adolescents' perceived academic competence

Melanie Stutz[1] and Beate Schwarz[2]

[1]Department of Psychology, University of Basel, Basel, Switzerland
[2]School of Applied Psychology, Zurich University of Applied Sciences, Winterthur, Switzerland

The purpose of this study was to examine how different aspects of paternal and maternal control behaviours influence the perceived academic competence of early adolescents indirectly via their engagement with school. The analyses are based on a longitudinal study with two waves that were separated by 12 months. The participants were 228 early adolescents (50.4% girls) with an average age of 11.62 years ($SD = .41$) at the outset. Structural equation modeling analyses using bootstrapping procedures revealed that parental supervision was indirectly related to the perceived academic competence of adolescents via their engagement with schools, whereas parental authoritarian control was only linked to engagement with school. The discussion focuses on the multifaceted nature of parental control and the importance of both parents for the academic success of adolescents.

In an economically globalized society such as Switzerland, the completion of secondary school has become important for adolescents in order to successfully enter the labour market. Thus, the identification of factors that influence school achievement is relevant. Personal factors seem to play an important role in school completion. Here, we focus on the early adolescents' perception of their academic competence. Various studies have shown that the perceived academic competence of students is related to school success and academic achievement

We thank the families who volunteered to participate in the study. This research was supported by grants [SNF 100013-116500/1; SNF 100014-132278/1] awarded by the Swiss National Science Foundation to the second author.

(Bronstein, Ginsburg, & Herrera, 2005; Marsh, Trautwein, Lüdtke, Köller, & Baumert, 2006; Wong, Wiest, & Cusick, 2002). However, perceived academic competence decreases from childhood to adolescence (Cantin & Boivin, 2004). Thus, early adolescence seems to be a vulnerable period of life with respect to perceived academic competence.

In addition, the relationship between parents and adolescents starts changing in early adolescence. For instance, adolescents attempt to gain more autonomy from their parents, who in turn keep track of the adolescents' activities by increasing their supervision and monitoring. Nevertheless, warmth and support in the adolescent-parent relationship are still important for a healthy development (Smetana, Campione-Barr, & Metzger, 2006). Given the significance of early adolescents' perceived academic competence for school achievement, the questions arise of how parents foster or hinder a healthy development in the academic domain during the transitional phase of early adolescence and whether fathers and mothers play different roles in this process.

Thus, the present study aims to examine parenting and its association with the academic development of early adolescents: specifically, we focus on the link between facets of parental control (supervision and authoritarian control) and the perceived academic competence of early adolescents. In addition, by differentiating between the parenting of mothers and fathers, the current study contributes to the ongoing discussion about gender-specific roles of parents.

Facets of parental control and perceived academic competence

In research on parenting, two main dimensions have been differentiated: acceptance/responsiveness and demandingness/control (Maccoby & Martin, 1983). In the following, we refer only to the control dimension, which has proved to be a multifaceted construct (Grolnick & Pomerantz, 2009). Grolnick and Pomerantz refined the dimension of control by distinguishing two major facets: one, parental behaviour aiming to restrict the autonomy of the child; and two, guidance of the child/provision of structure. The former refers to forms of parenting such as exerting pressure, intruding and being dominant, while the latter describes forms of parenting such as behavioural and firm control as well as supervision. In the present study, we investigated the facets of authoritarian control and supervision. This supervision element shares some similarities with monitoring, measured with the dimension of parental knowledge. In discussing a reinterpretation of the construct "monitoring", Kerr and Stattin (2000) argued that research on parenting behaviour must distinguish between parents having knowledge of their children's whereabouts and the way in which the parents obtain this knowledge. Supervision on a conceptual level does not only comprise the knowledge of parents but also encloses an active part, namely, how much effort they put into obtaining knowledge.

With respect to associations between parental control and perceived academic competence, studies have shown a positive link with supervision/strictness (Gray & Steinberg, 1999) and with behavioural control (Wang, Pomerantz, & Chen, 2007). In contrast, aspects of authoritarian control, such as punitive and harsh parenting were negatively associated with perceived academic competence (Bronstein et al., 2005; Putnick et al., 2008). Thus, we expected a positive association between perceived academic competence and supervision on the one hand, and a negative association with authoritarian control on the other.

However, it is not clear whether the associations between parenting and perceived academic competence are direct. Li, Lerner, and Lerner (2010) argued that parenting influences perceived academic competence only indirectly through increased engagement of the child with school, which encompasses, for instance, investment in school and positive emotions related to school (Appleton, Christenson, & Furlong, 2008; Li et al., 2010). While Li et al. (2010) showed that school engagement predicted school competence the study failed to find an association between parental monitoring and school engagement. However, engagement with school was shown to be associated with parental provision of rules and structures (Hirschfield & Gasper, 2011). Based on this, we expected that engagement with school would mediate the link between parental control and perceived academic competence.

The evidence for differences in maternal and paternal parenting is weak. Most studies on parenting referred to composite measures of maternal and paternal parenting, or focus only on maternal parenting (Russell & Saebel, 1997). In general, there is some evidence that mothers and fathers play different roles in the lives of their adolescent children (Larson & Richards, 1994). The few studies on parenting and academic competence that have differentiated between maternal and paternal influences have revealed inconsistent results. Some studies showed very similar effects of paternal or maternal control behaviour (Putnick et al., 2008; Grolnick & Ryan, 1989), others showed differences (McGrath & Repetti, 2000). With respect to the planned mediator in our analyses, school engagement, to our knowledge, to date, no study has investigated the difference between maternal and paternal influences.

The present study

The existing literature on associations between parental control and perceived academic competence has neither included different facets of parental control nor has it differentiated the effects of maternal and paternal parenting on the academic development of early adolescents. The present study aims to fill this gap by providing an integrative model of effects in a longitudinal design of both supervision and authoritarian control on academic competence, which is relevant for school achievement. Within this integrative model, engagement with school is considered to be a mediator between the two facets of parental control and perceived academic competence as measured a year later. Based on the assumption of Li et al. (2010), we expected that the link between maternal and paternal control and the perceived academic competence would be mediated by the engagement of early adolescents with school. More specifically, we expected a negative association between maternal and paternal authoritarian control and engagement with school, a positive association between maternal and paternal supervision and engagement with school and, in turn, a positive association between engagement with school and perceived academic competence. As little is known about differential effects of the control behaviour of mothers and fathers and its effects on academic competence, we intend to explore those differences.

METHOD

Procedure

The analyses are based on the second (2009) and third (2010) assessment of a longitudinal study in the German-speaking part of Switzerland. The majority of the families (77.3%) were recruited through their children's school in the city of Basel (Switzerland) and its surroundings. In addition, families were recruited through information provided by residents' registration offices (22.7% of the sample). The response rate was 17% on average.

Families were contacted for the first interview after returning a signed letter of consent. Trained interviewers conducted a two-hour standardized interview at the family's home, with the mother and the adolescent in separate rooms. For two-parent families, a questionnaire was left behind for the husband or the male partner to be completed and sent back by mail. Each family received 30 Swiss Francs (equivalent to 29 US Dollars) for participation.

Participants

In the current three-wave study, 246 fourth graders and their mothers participated in 2008, 228 mother-child dyads participated again in 2009 (attrition rate of 7.3%) and 208 two years later in 2010 (attrition rate of 8.8%). For the current analysis, we use data from 2009 and 2010. Thus, Time 1 refers to the year 2009 and Time 2 to the year 2010. Therefore, the analysis is based on 228 early adolescents.

The sample included 113 boys and 115 girls (age: $M = 11.62$ years; $SD = .41$ at Time 1). The majority of the parents were Swiss (82.9% mothers and 81.3% fathers), and the average age of the mothers was 42.35 years ($SD = 4.77$) and 45.05 years ($SD = 5.36$) for the fathers. With respect to education, 10.1% of the mothers and 6.1% of the fathers had only completed the nine years of compulsory education, a majority had finished formal job training (67.1% of the mothers and 52.5% of the fathers) and 22.8% of the mothers and 41.4% of the fathers had attained a university or college degree. Overall, the sample was biased toward more highly educated families and more Swiss nationals compared to the general population in Switzerland (Federal Statistical Office, 2011).

Measures

Measurement scales that were not available in German were independently translated by two members of the research team into German. The translations were discussed intensively within the team and revised when necessary. This procedure was developed by Van de Vijver and Leung (1997). The reliability and validity of the German versions were tested in a pilot study of 50 10-year-old children. Further, all measures used in the analyses are based on the adolescents' report only.

Parental supervision. At Time 1, maternal and paternal *supervision* was assessed with the German translation of a questionnaire of Lamborn, Mounts, Steinberg, and Dornbusch (1991). The four items of the subscale used in the analysis were divided into two parts, each leading to a separate indicator asking two different questions: "How important is it for your mother/father, to know . . ." and "How much does your mother/father REALLY know . . .". These two types of questions were asked regarding the parent knowing where the adolescent is after school and what she/he does during that time. All four items were rated on a four-point-Likert scale from 1 (*not important/not exactly*) to 4 (*very important/exactly*). The original scale was labelled supervision/strictness and included an additional aspect: the rules concerning time to come home at night (curfew). Due to the young age of the adolescents, in the present study, this was deemed not relevant and was omitted. Thus, we named the scale *supervision*. Internal consistency of the scale at Time 1 was $\alpha = .75$ for mothers and $\alpha = .87$ for fathers.

Parental authoritarian control. In 2009 (Time 1), to assess the *authoritarian control* of the parents, the early adolescents completed a subscale of the Parenting Practices Questionnaire (Robinson, Mandleco, Olson, & Hart, 1995). The early adolescents rated 11 items (e.g., "My mother/father threatens me, when she/he wants to punish me," Cronbach's $\alpha = .77$ for mothers and $\alpha = .79$ for fathers) ranging from 1 (*never*) to 5 (*very often*).

Early adolescents' engagement with school. Items of the School Enjoyment Scale (Fend, 1997) and the School Effort Scale (Fend, 1997) were used to assess engagement with school at Time 2. The School Enjoyment Scale was divided into two subscales, which we named school enjoyment and learning motivation.

To measure the early adolescents' school enjoyment four items were used (e.g., "I enjoy going to school"; $\alpha = .74$). For assessing learning motivation (e.g., "I am one of the students who enjoys learning"; $\alpha = .63$; ratings ranged from 1 (*strongly disagree*) to 5 (*strongly agree*)), we used two items. School effort was measured with three items (e.g., "How much of an effort do you put into school tasks?"; $\alpha = .73$ rated on a five-point-Likert-scale ranging from 1 (*none at all*) to 5 (*a lot*)) to get better internal consistency.

Perceived academic competence. To measure the perceived *academic competence* of early adolescents, the Self-Perception-Profile for Children (German version: Wünsche & Schneewind, 1989) was used at Time 1 and Time 2. The subscale included six items like "Some kids often forget what they learn ... but ... other kids can remember things easily." ($\alpha = .86$ at Time 1 and 2). According to the response format the adolescent picked the part of the statement that was most true and rated it on a two-point-scale 1 (*really true*) and 2 (*sort of true*) resulting in a four-point-scale with higher scores indicating higher perceived competence.

Strategy of analyses

To test the mediation mechanism between the parenting styles of fathers and mothers and the early adolescents' perceived academic competence, we used a structural equation modelling (SEM) framework and AMOS. Three latent constructs in the model, parental authoritarian control at Time 1, and perceived academic competence at Time 1 and 2 are composed of parcels a posteriori. When constructing, we tried to equally balance them in terms of discrimination using the item-total correlation. We matched the highest loaded item with the lowest within one parcel, the second highest with the second lowest in another parcel until all items were distributed.

Analyses were performed on the variance covariance matrix. Thus, missing values were excluded pairwise, which resulted in maximal $N = 216$. As the sample size did not allow for a comprehensive analysis we tested for mothers and fathers separately. Figure 1 shows the mediation models we tested. It implies that paternal and maternal supervision and authoritarian control measured at Time 1 have an effect on the perceived academic competence of the early adolescents at Time 2 both directly as well as indirectly through the early adolescents' engagement with school measured at Time 2. In order to control for potential autoregressive processes, perceived academic competence measured at Time 1 was included as a predictor. All constructs were modelled as latent variables. For parental supervision, the measurement errors of the importance of knowing where the early adolescent spends her/his spare time and the actual knowing of it were allowed to co-vary. In addition, covariances between the error terms of the indicators

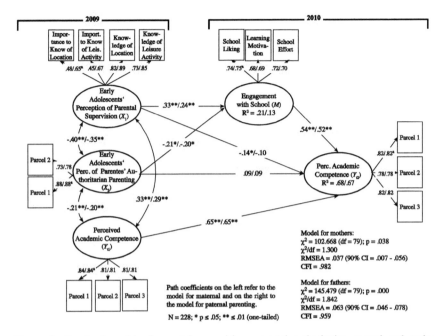

Figure 1. Structural model of parental supervision, parental authoritarian control and early adolescents' perceived academic competence at Time 1 and early adolescents' engagement with school and their perceived academic competence at Time 2. Standardized path coefficients are presented.

measuring the same aspect of perceived academic competence at Time1 and Time 2 were included. To test the mediating (indirect) effects, we used the bootstrap method (Preacher & Hayes, 2008) and 5000 bootstrap samples.

RESULTS

Table 1 contains the means, standard deviations and inter-correlations of all indicators in the study. Low to moderate correlations were found among the manifest variables.

The early adolescents' perception of parental control behaviour

First, we tested whether the early adolescents reported differences between paternal and maternal control behaviour. T-Tests for dependent samples revealed a significant effect for parental supervision ($t(218) = 8.243$, $p < .001$). Paternal supervision was perceived to be lower than maternal supervision. For authoritarian control, the t-tests did not show a significant difference between fathers and mothers.

TABLE 1
Intercorrelations and means (with standard deviations) for indicator variables

	1	2	3	4	5	6	7	8	9	10	11	12	13	14	15	16	17	18	19	20	21
1 Importance to Know of Leisure Activity (Mothers) t1	—																				
2 Importance to Know of Leisure Activity (Fathers) t1	.71[b]	—																			
3 Importance to Know of Location (Mothers) t1	.50[b]	.51[b]	—																		
4 Importance to Know of Location (Fathers) t1	.40[b]	.64[b]	.70[b]	—																	
5 Mothers' Knowl. of Activity t1	.41[b]	.44[b]	.34[b]	.34[b]	—																
6 Fathers' Knowl. of Activity t1	.35[b]	.59[b]	.37[b]	.58[b]	.71[b]	—															
7 Mothers' Knowl. of Location t1	.32[b]	.39[b]	.39[b]	.34[b]	.60[b]	.54[b]	—														
8 Fathers' Knowl. of Location t1	.28[b]	.53[b]	.41[b]	.61[b]	.44[b]	.76[b]	.66[b]	—													
9 Mothers' Author. Parenting P1 t1	−.11	−.19[b]	−.10	−.15[a]	−.32[b]	−.31[b]	−.23[b]	−.25[b]	—												
10 Fathers' Author. Parenting P1 t1	−.08	−.14[a]	−.04	−.13	−.26[b]	−.29[b]	−.21[b]	−.30[b]	.77[b]	—											
11 Mothers' Author. Parenting P2 t1	−.11	−.22[b]	−.06	−.11	−.33[b]	−.36[b]	−.22[b]	−.22[b]	.70[b]	.60[b]	—										
12 Fathers' Author. Parenting P2 t1	−.06	−.17[a]	.01	−.09	−.22[b]	−.29[b]	−.17[a]	−.22[b]	.52[b]	.71[b]	.75[b]	—									
13 School Liking t2	.13	.22[b]	.07	.05	.22[b]	.22[b]	.22[b]	.20[b]	−.13	−.13	−.21[b]	−.17[a]	—								
14 Learning Motivation t2	.15[a]	.16[a]	.11	.04	.12	.16[a]	.14[a]	.13	−.10	−.08	−.17[a]	−.13	.53[b]	—							
15 School Effort t2	.24[b]	.26[b]	.15[a]	.07	.32[b]	.24[b]	.26[b]	.16[a]	−.22[b]	−.19[b]	−.30[b]	−.30[b]	.49[b]	.51[b]	—						
16 Academic Competence P1 t1	.14[a]	.20[b]	.10	.11	.20[b]	.24[b]	.21[b]	.21[b]	−.13[a]	−.15[a]	−.16[a]	−.20[b]	.29[b]	.18[a]	.31[b]	—					
17 Academic Competence P2 t1	.18[b]	.23[b]	.18[b]	.17[a]	.25[b]	.26[b]	.20[b]	.19[b]	−.13[a]	−.11	−.19[b]	−.18[b]	.28[b]	.13[a]	.31[b]	.68[b]	—				
18 Academic Competence P3 t1	.10	.12	.04	.02	.18[b]	.18[b]	.14[a]	.15[a]	−.06	−.04	−.14[a]	−.08	.23[b]	.10	.25[b]	.69[b]	.66[b]	—			
19 Academic Competence P1 t2	.02	.07	.04	−.05	.15[a]	.15[a]	.12	.10	−.11	−.06	−.20[b]	−.14	.50[b]	.37[b]	.43[b]	.55[b]	.50[b]	.47[b]	—		
20 Academic Competence P2 t2	.12	.12	.13	.10	.19[b]	.21[b]	.17[a]	.14	−.06	−.05	−.20[b]	−.21[b]	.40[b]	.26[b]	.44[b]	.50[b]	.59[b]	.49[b]	.65[b]	—	
21 Academic Competence P3 t2	.08	.14	.07	.03	.15[a]	.20[b]	.13	.10	−.01	−.02	−.11	−.11	.42[b]	.30[b]	.34[b]	.50[b]	.49[b]	.52[b]	.70[b]	.69[b]	—
M	3.14	2.84	3.45	3.18	3.28	3.02	3.47	3.12	1.88	1.79	2.00	2.05	3.73	2.72	3.73	3.12	3.11	3.12	2.94	3.05	3.13
SD	.76	.89	.74	.91	.81	.93	.74	1.00	.57	.55	.55	.57	.96	1.13	.74	.66	.67	.65	.65	.65	.65

Analysis of the mediation mechanism

Figure 1 illustrates our models to assess the mediating role of engagement with school with respect to effects of paternal and maternal control behaviour on the adolescents' perceived academic competence. Prior to testing the two models with maternal and paternal parenting, we examined the measurement structure of both models. First, as measurement invariance of constructs assessed at multiple time points is of importance, we tested perceived academic competence for metric invariance. We estimated a model with covariances between the two latent variables and fixed the variances of both latent variables to 1 (Kline, 2011). The likelihood ratio difference test was not significant ($\Delta\chi^2 = .401$, $\Delta df = 3$, $p = .940$), indicating that metric invariance across time was given for both models.

Second, when testing for the complete measurement structure of both models (mother and father) they showed an acceptable to good fit (model with maternal parenting: $\chi^2 = 89.640$, $df = 78$, $p = .173$; $\chi^2/df = 1.149$; $RMSEA = .026$ ($CI = .000-.048$); $CFI = .991$; model with paternal parenting: $\chi^2 = 129.919$, $df = 78$, $p < .001$; $\chi^2/df = 1.666$; $RMSEA = .056$ ($CI = .038-.072$); $CFI = .968$). In those models, the link between parental supervision and perceived academic competence of the early adolescents was positive (model for mothers: $r = .23$, $p = .006$, one-tailed; model for fathers: $r = .19$, $p = .008$, one-tailed), whereas the correlation between parental authoritarian control and the early adolescents' perceived academic competence was found to be negative (model for mothers: $r = -.16$, $p = .026$, one-tailed; model for fathers: $r = -.13$, $p = .052$, one-tailed).

The hypothesized models implying that Time 1 indicators of paternal and maternal control affect the perceived academic competence of the early adolescents at Time 2 through the engagement with school at Time 2 provided a good fit for the model with maternal parenting ($\chi^2 = 102.668$, $df = 79$, $p = .380$; $\chi^2/df = 1.300$; $RMSEA = .037$ ($CI = .009-.056$); $CFI = .982$) and an acceptable fit for the model with paternal parenting ($\chi^2 = 145.479$, $df = 79$, $p < .001$; $\chi^2/df = 1.842$; $RMSEA = .063$ ($CI = .046-.078$); $CFI = .959$).

Figure 1 illustrates the model with standardized parameter estimates for fathers and mothers obtained by the maximum likelihood estimation method. Unstandardized estimates of the structural part of the model are shown in Table 2. With respect to the first part of the mediational process, we found that both maternal and paternal supervision were positively linked to the early adolescents' engagement with school, whereas maternal and paternal authoritarian control were negatively linked to school engagement.

In summary, the higher the perceived level of parental supervision, and the lower the perceived level of parents' authoritarian control, the higher the engagement with school one year later. These associations were statistically significant. As predicted, engagement with school was linked positively and

TABLE 2
Unstandardized parameter estimates of direct and indirect effects

Model for Mothers

Effect	Estimate	SE	p*
Direct effects			
$X_1 \rightarrow M$	.640	.205	.001
$X_2 \rightarrow M$	−.286	.134	.016
$X_1 \rightarrow Y_{t2}$	−.198	.070	.039
$X_2 \rightarrow Y_{t2}$	.090	.112	.101
$M \rightarrow Y_{t2}$	.389	.062	.000
$Y_{t1} \rightarrow Y_{t2}$	.605	.058	.000

		95% Bootstrap CI	
	Estimate	LL	UL
Simple indirect effect			
$X_1 \rightarrow M \rightarrow Y_{t2}$	.249	.088	.521
$X_2 \rightarrow M \rightarrow Y_{t2}$	−.111	−.227	.088
Total indirect effect			
$X_1 \rightarrow Y_{t2}$	.051	−.181	.298
$X_2 \rightarrow Y_{t2}$	−.022	−.197	.126

Model for Fathers

Effect	Estimate	SE	p*
Direct effects			
$X_1 \rightarrow M$	.298	.112	.004
$X_2 \rightarrow M$	−.283	−.130	.015
$X_1 \rightarrow Y_{t2}$	−.092	.060	.068
$X_2 \rightarrow Y_{t2}$	.091	.067	.855
$M \rightarrow Y_{t2}$	.366	.056	.000
$Y_{t1} \rightarrow Y_{t2}$	.601	.057	.000

		95% Bootstrap CI	
	Estimate	LL	UL
Simple indirect effect			
$X_1 \rightarrow M \rightarrow Y_{t2}$	.109	.020	.209
$X_2 \rightarrow M \rightarrow Y_{t2}$	−.104	−.231	.36
Total indirect effect			
$X_1 \rightarrow Y_{t2}$	.017	−.111	.149
$X_2 \rightarrow Y_{t2}$	−.013	−.166	.128

Notes: SE = standard error; CI = confidence interval. *one-tailed.
X_1 Paternal Monitoring at T1. X_2 Paternal Authoriatrian control at T1. *Y* Academic Competence at T1 and T2. *M* School Engagement at T2.

significantly in both models with perceived academic competence, which indicates that the higher the engagement with school, the higher the adolescents' perceived academic competence. Except for the negative direct effect of maternal supervision, all direct effects of parenting on perceived academic competence were not significant.

The model consists of two indirect effects (e.g., $X_1 \rightarrow M \rightarrow Y_{t2}$), each composed of two direct effects and two total effects (i.e., the sum of the total indirect effect and the direct effect; e.g., $X_1 \rightarrow Y_{t2}$). Table 2 shows the point and bootstrap interval estimates of these effects. The indirect effects, which connect maternal and paternal supervision with perceived academic competence through school engagement, were positive and statistically significant (two-tailed) for mothers and fathers as the bootstrap confidence limit excludes 0. In contrast, the total effects between those variables were not significant (two-tailed) suggesting the link between parental supervision and perceived academic competence is fully mediated through school engagement.

With respect to the indirect effects, which connect maternal and paternal authoritarian control with perceived academic competence via school engagement, the estimates were both negative and statistically not significant (two-tailed). Likewise, the total effect was negative and not significant (two-tailed). Thus, the analyses provided evidence for school engagement serving as a mediator between supervision and perceived academic competence, but not between authoritarian parenting and perceived academic competence.

DISCUSSION

The present study aimed to investigate the effects of different facets of paternal and maternal control on the perceived academic competence of early adolescents. Given the importance of the expanding field of research on the roles of fathers and mothers in child rearing, this study contributes to the ongoing debate on paternal and maternal parenting and its impact on a child's development, in particular in the academic domain. There have been theoretical discussions proposing that the link between parenting and academic competence is not direct but mediated through engagement with school (Li et al., 2010). Thus, we tested this model, conducting structural equation analysis encompassing data of two waves of a longitudinal study.

The structural equation model partially corroborated our expectation that paternal and maternal control exert their influence indirectly through the engagement of early adolescents with school. This hypothesis held for parental supervision. Paternal and maternal supervision increased the early adolescents' engagement with school. Lower engagement with school, in turn, led to lower perceived academic competence. This finding is in accordance with the theoretical assumptions of Li et al. (2010), but not with their results. In that study, the authors failed to show a mediation effect. This incongruence may be a result of the different operationalization of the constructs used in the studies. In contrast to our study, their measure of monitoring comprised only knowledge items and their measures of school engagement differentiated between emotional and behavioural school engagement. Thus, to gain a deeper understanding of this mediation mechanism more studies using the same measurements for the constructs are needed.

Although the direct effects between fathers' and mothers' authoritarian control and school engagement, as well as later and perceived academic competence were statistically significant, the bootstrapping procedures revealed the indirect effect to not be statistically significant. Using bootstrapping procedures led to missing cases being excluded from the analyses, reducing the sample power. We used the covariance matrix for the estimation, thus normality of the data is only assumed and the estimates are not as reliable as the estimates obtained from observed data. Since we did not want to lose further power for the analysis we decided against the use of raw data because it would have required excluding cases listwise. Nevertheless, based on this result, we draw the careful conclusion that authoritarian control of fathers and mothers is related to lower school engagement. School engagement in turn is also a relevant personal characteristic for success in school (e.g., Appleton et al., 2008). Therefore, the present study underlines that harsh parenting of both fathers and mothers is unfavourable for the functioning of adolescents in school. In sum, in early adolescence, different facets of parental control lead to different outcomes concerning the child's academic accomplishments. Parental guidance and structure exert a positive effect, whereas punitive and harsh parenting hinders good development.

The analyses showed an unexpected negative effect of maternal supervision on perceived academic competence. However, when testing the measurement models, the correlation between these two constructs was positive. The negative effect only occurs when the association is controlled for other constructs in the model, which suggests a suppressor effect. Therefore, we do not want to overestimate this result.

The positive link between maternal and paternal supervision and engagement with school is in agreement with a similar finding by Hirschfield and Gasper (2011) and adds to the rare studies on the effects of parental supervision on adolescent academic development (for a review, please see Crouter & Head, 2002). However, recent research on the construct of monitoring has shown that parental knowledge, which was a main component of our supervision scale, is gained more frequently by adolescent behaviour such as self-disclosure then through parental effort (Kerr & Stattin, 2000). Further, supervision indicators without knowledge items revealed weaker associations with adolescents' psycho-social adjustment than indicators including these items (Kerr, Stattin, & Özdemir, 2012). These results point to an important role of the adolescent within this process. Nevertheless, based on studies that have shown that parental competence in serving as an attachment figure and providing a climate of trust (see Crouter & Head, 2002) is a necessary base for adolescent self-disclosure, we can conclude that parents who are able to create a family climate in which knowledge about the whereabouts of the adolescents is shared support the academic development of their adolescents.

Further, paternal and maternal authoritarian control was associated with lower engagement with school. To our knowledge, this is the first study that provides evidence for this link. Nevertheless, it corroborates findings on negative links between punitive parenting and "persistence, goal-directed behaviour, and performance with respect to academic endeavours" (Linder Gunnoe, Hetherington, & Reiss, 2006, p. 592).

Unlike most studies on parenting, the present study differentiated between paternal and maternal control behaviour. Although we could not integrate maternal and paternal control behaviour into one model due to the small sample size, this study underlines that both mothers and fathers play an important role in the early adolescents' perception of their academic competence. This is in accordance with previous studies, which have demonstrated similar influences of mothers and fathers on the perceived academic or cognitive competence of adolescents (Grolnick & Ryan, 1989; Putnick et al., 2008). Given that paternal involvement in parenting has long been neglected in most developmental research, it is important to underline that fathers are as relevant as mothers in the academic success of their adolescents. Nevertheless, further research is needed before we can draw firm conclusions about the influence of paternal control on the child's development.

Although the longitudinal design of our study is comprehensive, it is not without limitations. First, the current study was based on only two times of assessment, and the association between engagement with school and perceived academic competence was tested cross-sectionally (at Time 2); therefore, the causal direction of this association remains unclear. Second, the results of our study may only be generalizable to well-educated and relatively well-functioning families. Replications of our findings with other families (e.g., families with lower socio-economic status, with higher levels of distress) would be useful, in particular with respect to the effects of parenting on academic development. Third, all indicators were assessed from the perspective of the adolescent. Correlations between indicators reported by parents and the adolescents were very low and did not allow for including multiple perspectives into one latent construct. This may lead to an overestimation of associations. However, particularly in adolescence, the child's perception of parenting might have a stronger impact than actual parental behaviour.

The aim of the current study was to broaden our knowledge on the influence of different facets of paternal and maternal control on the academic development of early adolescents. The results stress the importance of the role of both parents in their child's development. In addition depending on the control behaviour facet, it may hinder or support the development of the early adolescents. Thus, the competence of both parents in adequate supervision should be supported and alternatives for harsh and punitive parenting should be offered to fathers and mothers.

REFERENCES

Appleton, J. J., Christenson, S. L., & Furlong, M. J. (2008). Student engagement with school: Critical conceptual and methodological issues of the construct. *Psychology in the Schools, 45,* 369–386.

Bronstein, P., Ginsburg, G. S., & Herrera, I. S. (2005). Parental predictors of motivational orientation in early adolescence: A longitudinal study. *Journal of Youth and Adolescence, 34,* 559–575.

Cantin, S., & Boivin, M. (2004). Change and stability in children's social network and self-perception during transition from elementary to junior high school. *International Journal of Behavioral Development, 28,* 561–570.

Crouter, A. C., & Head, M. R. (2002). Parental monitoring and knowledge of children. In M. Bornstein (Ed.), *Handbook of parenting 2nd ed., vol. 3: Becoming and being a parent* (pp. 461–483). Mahwah, NJ: Erlbaum.

Federal Statistical Office. (2011). *Bildungsstand* [Educational background]. Retrieved from: http://www.bfs.admin.ch/bfs/portal/de/index/themen/15/01/key/blank/01.html

Fend, H. (1997). *Der Umgang mit Schule in der Adoleszenz* [Dealing with school in adolescence]. Bern: Hans Huber.

Gray, M. R., & Steinberg, L. (1999). Unpacking authoritative parenting: Reassessing a multidimensional construct. *Journal of Marriage and the Family, 61,* 574–587.

Grolnick, W. S., & Pomerantz, E. M. (2009). Issues and challenges in studying parental control: Toward a new conceptualization. *Child Development Perspectives, 3,* 165–170.

Grolnick, W. S., & Ryan, R. M. (1989). Parent styles associated with children's self-regulation and competence in school. *Journal of Educational Psychology, 81,* 143–154.

Hirschfield, P. J., & Gasper, J. (2011). The relationship between school engagement and delinquency in late childhood and early adolescence. *Journal of Youth and Adolescence, 40,* 3–22.

Kerr, M., & Stattin, H. (2000). What parents know, how they know it, and several forms of adolescent adjustment: Further support for a reinterpretation of monitoring. *Developmental Psychology, 36,* 366–380.

Kerr, M., Stattin, H., & Özdemir, M. (2012). Perceived parenting style and adolescent adjustment: Revisiting directions of effects and the role of parental knowledge. *Developmental Psychology, 48,* 1540–1553.

Kline, R. B. (2011). *Principles and practice of structural equation modeling* (3rd ed.). New York, NY: Guilford.

Lamborn, S. D., Mounts, N. S., Steinberg, L., & Dornbusch, S. M. (1991). Patterns of competence and adjustment among adolescents from authoritative, authoritarian, indulgent, and neglectful families. *Child Development, 62,* 1049–1065.

Larson, R., & Richards, M. H. (1994). *Divergent realities. The emotional lives of mothers, fathers, and adolescents.* New York, NY: Basic Books.

Li, Y., Lerner, J. V., & Lerner, R. M. (2010). Personal and ecological assets and academic competence in early adolescence: The mediating role of school engagement. *Journal of Youth and Adolescence, 39,* 801–815.

Linder Gunnoe, M., Hetherington, M. E., & Reiss, D. (2006). Differential impact of fathers' authoritarian parenting on early adolescent adjustment in conservative protestant versus other families. *Journal of Family Psychology, 20,* 589–596.

Maccoby, E. E., & Martin, J. A. (1983). Socialization in the context of the family: Parent-child interaction. In P. H. Mussen (Ed.), *Handbook of child psychology* (Vol. IV, 4th ed.) (pp. 1–101). New York, NY: John Wiley & Sons.

Marsh, H. W., Trautwein, U., Lüdtke, O., Köller, O., & Baumert, J. (2006). Integration of multidimensional self-concept and core personality constructs: Construct validation and relations to well-being and achievement. *Journal of Personality, 74,* 403–456.

McGrath, E. P., & Repetti, R. L. (2000). Mothers' and fathers' attitudes toward their children's academic performance and children's perceptions of their academic competence. *Journal of Youth and Adolescence, 29*, 713–723.

Preacher, K. J., & Hayes, A. (2008). Asymptotic and resampling strategies for assessing and comparing indirect effects in multiple mediator models. *Behavior Research Methods, 40*, 879–891.

Putnick, D. L., Bornstein, M. H., Collins, A. W., Hendricks, C., Painter, K. M., & Suwalsky, J. T. D. (2008). Parenting stress, perceived parenting behaviors, and adolescent self-concept in European American families. *Journal of Family Psychology, 22*, 752–762.

Robinson, C. C., Mandleco, B., Olson, S. F., & Hart, C. H. (1995). Authoritative, authoritarian, and permissive parenting practices: Development of a new measure. *Psychological Reports, 77*, 819–830.

Russell, A., & Saebel, J. (1997). Mother-son, mother-daughter, father-son, and father-daughter: Are they distinct relationships? *Developmental Review, 17*, 111–147.

Smetana, J. G., Campione-Barr, N., & Metzger, A. (2006). Adolescent development in interpersonal and societal contexts. *Annual Review of Psychology, 57*, 255–284.

SPSS Amos. (20.0). [Computer software]. http://www-03.ibm.com/software/products/en/spss-amos

Van de Vijver, F. J. R., & Leung, K. (1997). *Methods and data analysis for cross cultural research*. Thousand Oaks, CA: Sage.

Wang, Q., Pomerantz, E. M., & Chen, H. (2007). The role of parents' control in early adolescents' psychological functioning: A longitudinal investigation in the United States and China. *Child Development, 78*, 1592–1610.

Wong, E. H., Wiest, D. J., & Cusick, L. B. (2002). Perceptions of autonomy support, parent attachement, competence and self-worth as predictors of motivational orientation and academic achievement: An examination of sixth- and ninth-grade regular education students. *Adolescence, 37*, 255–266.

Wünsche, P., & Schneewind, K. A. (1989). Entwicklung eines Fragebogens zur Erfassung von Selbst- und Kompetenzeinschätzungen bei Kindern (FSK-K) [Development of a questionnaire on perception of self and competence of children]. *Diagnostica, 35*, 217–235.

113

Couples' evaluations of fatherhood in different stages of the family life cycle

Franziska Fuhrmans, Holger von der Lippe, and Urs Fuhrer

Department of Psychology, Otto-von-Guericke-University Magdeburg, Germany

Fathers' and mothers' views on mothers' satisfaction with paternal behaviour as well as the respective processes of origination were studied in 393 cohabiting couples from three different stages of the family life cycle. Data on paternal competence and the couples' relationship characteristics were included as predictors in multiple regression analyses, and the stages of the family life cycle were taken into account with multigroup regression analyses. Results showed that the mothers were more satisfied with paternal behaviour than the fathers thought the mothers were. Moreover, mothers were satisfied when the fathers were willing to spend time with the child, whereas fathers thought that their partners were satisfied when they were able to establish and maintain a relationship with the child. Couple relationship satisfaction had a consistent impact on fathers' views, whereas it was not relevant to mothers' views unless the oldest child had reached adolescence.

Fatherhood is a complex phenomenon that is narrowly embedded in the proximal family system. Therefore, research on fatherhood involves much more than just the father himself. For a considerable time now, there has been evidence of spillover processes between the couple relationship and the parent–child relationship (Erel & Burman, 1995). Moreover, there seem to be crossover processes such that the marital satisfaction of one partner influences the parenting practices of the other partner.

Pedro, Ribeiro, and Shelton (2012) detected a stronger dependency of fathers' parenting practices on mothers' marital satisfaction than vice versa. This finding is consistent with the fathering vulnerability hypothesis, which asserts that the negative influence of lower marital satisfaction on parenting behaviour is stronger for fathers than it is for mothers (Cummings, Merrilees, & George, 2010). Pedro et al. (2012) point to the coparenting relationship as a mediator between the marital satisfaction of one partner and the parenting practices of the other partner. Bonney, Kelly, and Levant (1999) found that the relation between mothers' perceptions of paternal competence and the amount of father involvement is mediated by marital satisfaction; Fagan and Barnett (2003) referred to maternal gatekeeping as a mediating variable between mothers' perceptions of paternal competence and the amount of father involvement. Maternal gatekeeping is thereby defined as mothers closing the gates on fathers' involvement, but it likewise includes mothers opening the gates to support fathers' involvement (Schoppe-Sullivan, Brown, Cannon, Mangelsdorf, & Szewczyk Sokolowski, 2008). With the latter meaning, the construct of maternal gatekeeping expands the fathering vulnerability hypothesis by providing a resource perspective. Thus, research needs to examine how mothers and fathers communicate their perceptions and come to shape each other's perception (Tremblay & Pierce, 2011). McBride et al. (2005) found that mothers' perceptions of paternal involvement, but not fathers' own perceptions, were related to paternal involvement. It is an open question, however, on how these perceptions are formed. The present study addresses some of these research requirements by considering dyadic data on mothers' perspectives on fatherhood.

MOTHERS' SATISFACTION WITH PATERNAL BEHAVIOUR

Mothers' satisfaction with paternal behaviour—and the father's perception of the mother's satisfaction with his behaviour—might be crucial variables for research on how mothers and fathers negotiate fatherhood and how fatherhood is embedded in the couple's relationship (Kulik & Tsoref, 2010). DeLuccie (1995) found that the indirect effect of marital satisfaction on the frequency of father involvement, as it was mediated by mothers' satisfaction with father involvement, was stronger than the direct effect. Similarly, Simmerman, Blacher, and Baker (2001) found that mothers' satisfaction with fathers' help in families with young children with a disability was more strongly related to the families' well-being than was the actual overall amount of fathers' help.

Overall, the recent literature points towards mothers' satisfaction with paternal behaviour as a crucial variable for fatherhood research. To our knowledge, no previous studies have provided dyadic data on mothers' satisfaction with paternal behaviour. Such data might, however, be useful for an exploration of how fathers' and mothers' perceptions of fatherhood concur or differ and thereby shed light on the couple's negotiations concerning fatherhood.

COUPLE RELATIONSHIP SATISFACTION

DeLuccie (1995) empirically demonstrated that marital relationship is a potential predictor of mothers' satisfaction with paternal behaviour, whereas Simmerman et al. (2001) showed the reverse effect such that mothers' satisfaction with fathers' involvement contributed to marital adjustment. The latter authors concluded that the direction of influence was still unclear and suggested that the relation between mothers' satisfaction with fathers' involvement and marital satisfaction be considered further by dyadic assessments of these variables. Krishnakumar and Black (2003) also pointed to relationship satisfaction as a potential predictor of mothers' satisfaction with paternal behaviour and declared that parenting efficacy was a moderator of that relation. These studies all provide evidence that relationship satisfaction is a relevant predictor of mothers' satisfaction with paternal behaviour.

PATERNAL COMPETENCE

In addition to the relationship satisfaction of both partners, paternal competence has been thought to contribute to mothers' satisfaction with paternal behaviour. This assumption was confirmed by Tremblay and Pierce (2011), who found in a longitudinal study that fathers' parental self-efficacy when the child was 2 months old significantly predicted mothers' perceptions of paternal competence and of the amount of father involvement when the child was 5 months old. Because a father's parental self-efficacy can be understood as a self-rating of paternal competence and because mothers' perceptions of this paternal competence and of the amount of paternal involvement are thought to be related to mothers' satisfaction with paternal behaviour, we considered paternal competence as a possible predictor of mothers' satisfaction with paternal behaviour. Another reason to address paternal competence as a potential predictor of mothers' satisfaction with paternal behaviour can be found in the study by Cannon, Schoppe-Sullivan, Mangelsdorf, Brown, and Szewczyk Sokolowski (2008), who found reciprocal relations between maternal gate-keeping and fathering behaviour.

THE PRESENT STUDY

One aim of this study was to explore mothers' satisfaction with paternal behaviour from mothers' as well as fathers' points of view and to consider possible differences within the couple. Fathers may tend to underestimate their partners' satisfaction with paternal behaviour because, even today, fathers may still feel some uncertainty about their fathering role (Daly, Ashbourne, & Brown, 2009). Clarification of this issue would make a worthwhile contribution to research on fatherhood and could provide deeper insight into the mutual influences within the couple concerning fatherhood.

Another aim of the present study was to explore the origination of fathers' and mothers' views on mothers' satisfaction with paternal behaviour. This process is of particular interest because it may reveal possible conflicts within coparenting couples. If the self-assessment and the external assessment (i.e., by fathers) of mothers' satisfaction with paternal behaviour are based on different variables, this discrepancy could be an indication of problems in the interpersonal adjustment of mutual expectations about what a good father is like. The existing literature refers to couple relationship characteristics and to paternal competence as possible predictors of mothers' satisfaction with paternal behaviour, but it does not provide any information on how relevant these predictors are for fathers' versus mothers' perceptions.

In addition, another objective of the present study was to consider elementary knowledge from family research. Taking into account the idea that the family system in which fatherhood is embedded changes over time, one can conclude that fatherhood changes too as do mothers' satisfaction with fatherhood from both parents' perspectives and the origination of these perceptions of fatherhood. Therefore, the particular importance of various predictors of mothers' satisfaction with paternal behaviour may vary between different stages of the family life cycle.

HYPOTHESES AND RESEARCH GOALS

We had three hypotheses:

(1) There will be significant mean-level differences between fathers' and mothers' ratings of mothers' satisfaction with paternal behaviour.

(2a) Mothers' satisfaction with paternal behaviour will be predicted by couple relationship characteristics as well as by mothers' perceptions of paternal competence.

(2b) Fathers' ratings of mothers' satisfaction with paternal behaviour will be predicted by couple relationship characteristics as well as by self-perceived paternal competence.

Besides these hypotheses, we explored:

(3) whether the self-ratings and the external ratings of mothers' satisfaction with paternal behaviour would be based on different variables.

Furthermore, we examined:

(4) whether there would be differences in the relevance of the predictors of mothers' satisfaction with paternal behaviour between various stages of family development for both self- and external assessments of mothers' satisfaction with paternal behaviour.

METHOD

Participants and procedure

Participants were recruited through day care centres and elementary and secondary schools in the capital city of Saxony-Anhalt, Germany. Eligibility criteria were defined to include only couples (a) who had an oldest child between 3 and 5 years (day care centres), 6 and 10 years (elementary schools) or 11 and 15 years (secondary schools); (b) who lived together with this oldest child in one household (either married or in cohabitation) and (c) of whom both members were willing to participate.

Data collection took place between the years 2009 and 2010. Forty-four institutions were included, and 4525 couples were addressed via parents' letters. Seventeen percent of these addressed couples gave their agreement to participate so that 756 sets of questionnaires were distributed. The rate of complete and acceptable questionnaire returns was 48%. These 364 couples were supplemented by 72 couples who also complied with the eligibility criteria and were recruited through eight elementary schools in a preceding survey, which took place in the year 2008. The entire sample consisted of 436 couples. For this study, 393 couples without missing values on the variables used for the present analyses were included.

The sample was divided into three subsamples: first subsample, 109 couples with an oldest child between the ages of 3 and 5; second subsample, 123 couples with an oldest child between the ages of 6 and 10 and third subsample, 161 couples with an oldest child between the ages of 11 and 15. The age of the oldest child is commonly used to define the family's developmental stage (Palkovitz, 2002). The average age of fathers from the first, second and third subsamples was 35, 37 and 42 years (SD = 6.32/4.70/5.22), respectively; the age of the respective partners was 32, 35 and 39 years (SD = 5.13/4.37/3.78), respectively. Mothers as well as fathers were employed in 66% of the first, 73% of the second and 82% of the third subsamples. Both parents had a German nationality in 93% of all samples. Percentages of parents from the first, second and third subsamples with only one child were 46%, 46% and 39% and two children were 49%, 42% and 53%, respectively. The level of education was approximately representative with respect to the ages of the parents and children as well as the types of institutions through which the couples were recruited.

Measures

Questionnaires included 275 items for fathers and 173 items for mothers. For the present analyses, mothers' and fathers' ratings of mothers' satisfaction with paternal behaviour were chosen as outcome variables, and aspects of the father–child relationship and the couple relationship were included as predictors.

Mothers' and fathers' ratings of mothers' satisfaction with paternal behaviour. These ratings were operationalized as single-item measures (i.e., "How satisfied are you with your partner's fathering behaviour?" and "How satisfied do you think your partner is with your fathering behaviour?"). Mothers and fathers rated mothers' global satisfaction with paternal behaviour via 5-point Likert scales ranging from 1 (*not satisfied*) to 5 (*very satisfied*).

Paternal competence. The father–child relationship was operationalized by six scales from the Constance Father Inventory (Wenger-Schittenhelm & Walter, 2002). These scales consist of overall paternal competence (10 items), patience in contact with the child (10 items), willingness to spend time with the child (10 items), the ability to establish and maintain a relationship with the child (eight items), assertiveness in the relationship with the child (seven items) and the extent to which the father grants autonomy to the child (seven items). The original item wordings were used for fathers, and modified wordings were used for mothers; they were rated via 5-point Likert scales. With respect to Wenger-Schittenhelm and Walter (2002), in the present data, we found similarly high reliability coefficients ranging from Cronbach's $\alpha = .85$ for the self-perceived extent to which the father grants autonomy to the child up to .93 for self-perceived patience in contact with the child. We found values of $\alpha = .90$ for the mother's perception of the extent to which the father grants autonomy to the child up to .94 for the mother's perception of global paternal competence. Wenger-Schittenhelm and Walter (2002) demonstrated the factorial validity of the Constance Father Inventory. The required factor structure was replicated in the present study too.

Couple relationship satisfaction. Aspects of the couple relationship were operationalized by single-item measures for both fathers and mothers ("How satisfied are you with your relationship?") and rated on a 5-point Likert scale. Noyon and Kock (2006) reported that single-item measures of relationship satisfaction have been shown to be valid measures of relationship satisfaction in diverse studies. Therefore, the use of a single item to measure relationship satisfaction is justified, especially with respect to demands for economy on questionnaires. We also used another single-item measure for fathers' feeling of constraint ("Do you feel constrained by your partner with respect to your fathering behaviour?") rated on a 5-point Likert scale.

RESULTS

Intra- and interpersonal correlation matrices are shown in Table 1. For mothers as well as fathers, all variables were correlated significantly and in a meaningful

TABLE 1
Intra- and interpersonal correlations among the main variables

Measure	1	2	3	4	5	6	7	8	9
(a) Intrapersonal correlations (mothers' views below and fathers' views above the principal diagonal)									
1. Mother's satisfaction with father	1	.555***	.387***	.464***	.474***	.234***	.269***	.447***	.341***
2. Father's global competence	.772***	1	.567***	.638***	.631***	.278***	.409***	.235***	−.192***
3. Father's patience with child	.493***	.660***	1	.588***	.635***	.293***	.560***	.151**	−.215***
4. Father's time for child	.646***	.745***	.586***	1	.711***	.331***	.510***	.219***	−.265***
5. Father's relationship with child	.588***	.749***	.689***	.708***	1	.292***	.616***	.163**	−.202***
6. Father's assertiveness with child	.334***	.400***	.251***	.331***	.253***	1	.365***	.198***	−.192***
7. Father's autonomy granting to child	.447***	.543***	.568***	.461***	.558***	.370***	1	.132**	−.181***
8. Couple relationship satisfaction	.549***	.641***	.451***	.444***	.433***	.394***	.393***	1	−.368***
9. Father's feeling of being constrained	–	–	–	–	–	–	–	–	1
(b) Interpersonal correlations (mothers' views in the rows and fathers' views in the columns)									
1. Mother's satisfaction with father	.398***	.267***	.110	.226***	.232***	.121*	.112*	.278***	−.245***
2. Father's global competence	.447***	.369***	.235***	.288***	.359***	.166**	.178***	.295***	−.194***
3. Father's patience with child	.352***	.338***	.495***	.262***	.397***	.128*	.279***	.211***	−.145**
4. Father's time for child	.439***	.337***	.233***	.443***	.361***	.143**	.160**	.223***	−.181***
5. Father's relationship with child	.431***	.362***	.302***	.326***	.505***	.121*	.245***	.177***	−.178***
6. Father's assertiveness with child	.225***	.112*	.029	.078	.119*	.536***	.103*	.325***	−.204***
7. Father's autonomy granting to child	.261***	.227***	.253***	.222***	.350***	.164**	.381***	.178***	−.172**
8. Couple relationship satisfaction	.349***	.255***	.131*	.130*	.169**	.194***	.105*	.512***	−.243***
9. Father's feeling of being constrained	–	–	–	–	–	–	–	–	–

Note: * $p < .05$; ** $p < .01$; *** $p < .001$.

manner (i.e., positive correlations except in the case of fathers' feeling of constraint).

As shown in the top part of Table 1, the strongest intrapersonal correlations for mothers' satisfaction with paternal behaviour were found for overall paternal competence for both mothers ($r = .772$) and fathers ($r = .555$). Fathers' couple relationship satisfaction was most strongly related to their rating of mothers' satisfaction with paternal behaviour ($r = .447$), whereas mothers' couple relationship satisfaction was most strongly related to their rating of overall paternal competence ($r = .641$). Finally, fathers' feeling of being constrained in their fathering behaviour by their partner was most strongly related to couple relationship satisfaction ($r = .368$).

The principal diagonal in the bottom part of Table 1 represents the agreement between mothers' and fathers' ratings in the form of correlations. We observed the strongest relations within this principal diagonal except for mothers' ratings of fathers' overall competence, which was more strongly related to fathers' view on mothers' satisfaction with paternal behaviour ($r = .447$) than to fathers' view on their overall competence ($r = .368$). Another exception was fathers' view on mothers' satisfaction with paternal behaviour, which was more strongly related to mothers' ratings of overall paternal competence ($r = .447$), fathers' willingness to spend time with the child ($r = .439$) and fathers' ability to establish and maintain a relationship with the child ($r = .431$) than to mothers' satisfaction with paternal behaviour ($r = .398$).

Mothers' and fathers' views on mothers' satisfaction with the paternal behaviour

Table 2 includes means and standard deviations as well as the results of paired t-tests for differences between mothers' and fathers' ratings. As can be seen in Table 2, couples differed significantly such that mothers had higher ratings than fathers on all variables except for couple relationship satisfaction.

The significant mean-level difference between mothers' and fathers' ratings of mothers' satisfaction with paternal behaviour showed the largest effect size of all, $t(392) = 8.84$, $p = .000$, $r = .41$, which can be identified as medium to large (Cohen, 1988, as cited in Field, 2009). Thus, Hypothesis 1 was supported by the finding that mothers were much more satisfied with paternal behaviour than fathers believed.

Mothers' satisfaction with paternal behaviour

Multiple regression analyses were performed to predict mothers' satisfaction with paternal behaviour. The developmental stage of the family was accounted for by applying a multigroup regression analysis. Thereby, differences in the parameter estimates between the three stages of family development could be

TABLE 2
Means for mothers' and fathers' ratings and results of paired *t*-tests

| | Rating | | | | |
	Mother	Father	*t*	df	ES *r*
Mother's satisfaction with paternal behaviour	4.12 (0.73)	3.77 (0.68)	8.84***	392	.41
Father's global competence	4.26 (0.67)	3.96 (0.58)	8.55***	392	.40
Father's patience	3.87 (0.87)	3.61 (0.83)	6.09***	392	.29
Father's willingness to spend time	3.92 (0.84)	3.62 (0.75)	7.20***	392	.34
Father's ability to establish and maintain a relationship	4.32 (0.77)	4.16 (0.74)	4.23***	392	.21
Father's assertiveness	3.90 (0.91)	3.79 (0.76)	2.82**	392	.14
Father's granting of autonomy	4.38 (0.69)	4.07 (0.63)	8.34***	392	.39
Couple relationship satisfaction	4.18 (0.81)	4.27 (0.78)	− 2.25*	392	.11
Feeling constrained by the partner		2.00 (0.80)	–	–	–

Notes: Standard deviations appear in parentheses below the means. ES *r*, effect size *r*, $\sqrt{t^2/(t^2 + df)}$ (Rosenthal, 1991 as cited in Field, 2009) with *r* = .10 small effect, *r* = .30 medium effect, *r* = .50 large effect (Cohen, 1988, as cited in Field, 2009).
* $p < .05$; ** $p < .01$; *** $p < .001$.

accounted for. A fully restricted model with all regression coefficients set equal between the three groups was the baseline model, and modification indices were used to select which regression coefficient should be set free to enhance the model fit. The resulting parameters are shown in Table 3.

The corresponding model fits the data very well ($\chi^2 = 16.770$, df = 13, $p = .210$, CFI = .990, RMSEA = .047, SRMR = .016). As can be seen in Table 3, 68%, 44% and 70% of the variance in mothers' satisfaction with paternal behaviour was explained by the predictors for mothers from the first, second and third subsamples, respectively. Therefore, Hypothesis 2a was supported by finding that mothers' satisfaction with paternal behaviour was predicted by couple relationship characteristics as well as by mothers' perceptions of paternal competence.

Results of the multigroup multiple regression analysis provided evidence that there were differences in the relevance of the predictors for mothers' satisfaction with paternal behaviour between the various stages of family development and thereby provided a hint for the answer to Research Question 4. As shown in Table 3, the Wald test of parameter constraints indicated that the relaxation of equality constraints on the regression coefficients of mothers' perceptions of paternal global competence in the second subsample and of mothers' perceptions of paternal willingness to spend time with the child as well as mothers' relationship satisfaction in the third subsample enhanced the model fit significantly.

TABLE 3
Results of multigroup multiple regression analyses for the prediction of mothers' satisfaction with paternal behaviour

Predictor	Oldest child is 3–5 years old			Oldest child is 6–10 years old			Oldest child is 11–15 years old		
	B	SE B	β	B	SE B	β	B	SE B	β
Mother's perception of father's global competence[a]	.741***	.071	.632	.488***	.094	.462	.741***	.071	.693
Mother's perception of father's patience with child	-.051	.038	-.061	-.051	.038	-.064	-.051	.038	-.060
Mother's perception of father's time for child[a]	.230***	.049	.266	.230***	.049	.277	.056	.057	.063
Mother's perception of father's relationship with child	-.025	.052	-.024	-.025	.052	-.029	-.025	.052	.25
Mother's perception of father's assertiveness with child	-.003	.029	-.004	-.003	.029	-.005	-.003	.029	-.004
Mother's perception of father's autonomy granting to child	.027	.043	.025	.027	.043	.029	.027	.043	.023
Mother's couple relationship satisfaction[a]	.032	.048	.033	.032	.048	.042	.161**	.056	.171
Father's couple relationship satisfaction	.027	.034	.028	.027	.034	.032	.027	.034	.028
Intercept	.018			1.038			.174		
R^2	.681			.443			.699		

Note: ** $p < .01$; *** $p < .001$.

[a] Wald test of parameter constraints indicates significant differences between the subsamples, 16.654(3), $p < .001$.

Results suggested that for mothers from the first and second subsamples, the perceptions of global paternal competence as well as paternal willingness to spend time with the child predicted their satisfaction with paternal behaviour, whereas for mothers from the third subsample, global paternal competence and mothers' relationship satisfaction predicted satisfaction with paternal behaviour.

Fathers' ratings of mothers' satisfaction with paternal behaviour

For the paternal multigroup multiple regression model, the fully restricted model with all regression coefficients set equal between the three groups fits the data very well $(\chi^2 = 20.963$, df $= 18$, $p = .281$, CFI $= .987$, RMSEA $= .035$, SRMR $= .027$). According to the modification indices, freeing parameter constraints was not necessary. Therefore, in contrast to the maternal multigroup multiple regression analysis, there were no differences in the relevance of the predictors for fathers' perceptions of mothers' satisfaction with paternal behaviour between the various stages of family development (Research Question 4). The amount of explained variance was 37% for the first, 47% for the second and 51% for the third subsamples as shown in Table 4. Thus, Hypothesis 2b was supported by the finding that fathers' ratings of mothers' satisfaction with paternal behaviour were predicted by couple relationship characteristics as well as by self-perceived paternal competence.

The corresponding regression coefficients for the prediction of fathers' views on mothers' satisfaction with paternal behaviour are shown in Table 4: self-rated overall paternal competence, self-rated ability to establish and maintain a relationship with the child, fathers' couple relationship satisfaction and the degree to which the father felt constrained in his paternal behaviour by his partner predicted fathers' views on mothers' satisfaction with paternal behaviour.

Differences in the process of origination of fathers' versus mothers' ratings of maternal satisfaction with paternal behaviour

Addressing Resarch Question 3, we find that for both mothers and fathers in all three stages of family development, global paternal competence was a significant predictor of the ratings of mothers' satisfaction with paternal behaviour. Besides global paternal competence, for mothers, the perception of the father's willingness to spend time with the child significantly contributed to the amount of explained variance in the first and second subsamples, whereas for fathers, it was the self-rated ability to establish and maintain a relationship with the child in all three subsamples. For mothers, relationship satisfaction was a significant predictor only in the third subsample, whereas for fathers, relationship satisfaction was a significant predictor in all three stages of family development.

TABLE 4

Results of multigroup multiple regression analyses for the prediction of fathers' ratings of mothers' satisfaction with paternal behaviour

Predictor	Oldest child is 3–5 years old			Oldest child is 6–10 years old			Oldest child is 11–15 years old		
	B	SE B	β	B	SE B	β	B	SE B	β
Self-rated paternal global competence	.377***	.063	.318	.377***	.063	.345	.377***	.063	.303
Self-rated patience with child	.017	.043	.021	.017	.043	.021	.017	.043	.020
Self-rated time for child	.049	.053	.054	.049	.053	.053	.049	.053	.056
Self-rated relationship with child	.168**	.058	.191	.168**	.058	.177	.168**	.058	.182
Self-rated assertiveness with child	.006	.037	.006	.006	.037	.006	.006	.037	.006
Self-rated autonomy granting to child	−.085	.054	−.079	−.085	.054	−.079	−.085	.054	−.080
Father's couple relationship satisfaction	.219***	.040	.233	.219***	.040	.250	.219***	.040	.266
Mother's couple relationship satisfaction	.062	.037	.065	.062	.037	.076	.062	.037	.077
Father's feeling of being constrained by his partner	−.110**	.035	−.126	−.110**	.035	−.111	−.110**	.035	−.147
Intercept	.656			.729			.701		
R^2	.372			.470			.508		

Note: ** $p < .01$; *** $p < .001$.

DISCUSSION

This study considered mothers' and fathers' points of view with regard to mothers' satisfaction with paternal behaviour. Couples in three different stages of the family life cycle were examined, and regression analyses confirmed the relevance of father–child and couple relationship characteristics for both parents' views on mothers' satisfaction with paternal behaviour. We found that mothers are more satisfied with the paternal behaviour of their partners than the fathers believe. This underestimation effect can be explained by differences in the origination of these views. Mothers refer to their views on the father's willingness to spend time with the child (in the first and second subsamples), whereas fathers take into account their ability to establish and maintain a relationship with the child (in all three subsamples) when evaluating mothers' satisfaction with paternal behaviour. The challenge of qualitatively valuable father involvement as reflected by the paternal view on the ability to establish and maintain a relationship with the child thereby seems to be harder to meet than the challenge of quantitatively valuable father involvement as reflected by the maternal view on the paternal willingness to spend time with the child. Therefore, fathers' ratings on the maternal satisfaction with the paternal behaviour may turn out lower than mothers'.

This finding parallels the historical progression of fatherhood research: mothers, in a way, seem to have retained the somewhat facile conceptualization of fatherhood in terms of directly noticeable activities between the father and child, the view that was the predominant variable in fatherhood research until Palkovitz emphasized the necessity of a broader conceptualization of fatherhood that included affective and cognitive forms of involvement (Palkovitz, 2002). In contrast, fathers appear to entertain a broader conceptualization of fatherhood that includes qualitative aspects of the relationship with the child (Brown, Mangelsdorf, & Neff, 2012). This difference points to general difficulties for evaluations of fatherhood from the mother's point of view as well as from researchers' perspectives. Research on fatherhood should therefore conceptualize fatherhood in the manner in which fathers themselves understand and evaluate it or at least should bear in mind that fathers might conceptualize fatherhood in ways that differ from the conceptualizations of mothers and researchers (e.g., Fuhrmans, von der Lippe, & Fuhrer, 2012; Matzner, 2004).

Concerning couples' negotiation processes with respect to fatherhood, on the one hand, we can conclude from our results that fathers who want to meet their partners' expectations or who want their partner to be satisfied with their paternal behaviour should enhance their global paternal competence as well as their willingness to spend time with their children when the oldest child is between 3 and 10 years old and should work on increasing mothers' relationship satisfaction when the oldest child is between 11 and 15 years old instead of improving their ability to establish and maintain a relationship with the child. On the other hand, mothers should develop a conceptualization of fatherhood that incorporates an appreciation of the qualitative aspects of the father–child relationship.

Along this line of reasoning, the present explanation has to do with what has been termed fathers' *entrance to the maternal garden* (Kulik & Tsoref, 2010). Some mothers seem to have ambivalent feelings about enhanced paternal involvement and "(...) find it difficult to give up their historically significant roles as the main expert on childrearing" (Cowan & Cowan, 1987, p. 168). Mothers who are acting as gatekeepers may therefore more or less consciously try to decrease the intensity of the father–child relationship to maintain their role as the expert on child-related topics. Our findings show that the degree to which fathers feel constrained by their partners is a significant predictor of their evaluation of mothers' satisfaction with their paternal behaviour, thus confirming the idea that maternal gatekeeping has a relevant effect on fathers.

Still another effect may account for the mean-level differences between fathers' and mothers' perceptions of mothers' satisfaction with paternal behaviour, namely real-ideal discrepancies. Fathers may have high standards for their fathering role, see greater discrepancies between real versus ideal fathering behaviour and therefore rate mothers' satisfaction with their involvement lower; mothers, in contrast, may hold low expectations of fathers because they see themselves as responsible for child-related tasks and therefore see smaller discrepancies between real versus ideal fathering behaviour and, for this reason, state that they have higher satisfaction with paternal behaviour.

Furthermore, in the context of couples' negotiation processes, we found that relationship satisfaction was a significant predictor of fathers' evaluations of mothers' satisfaction with paternal behaviour in all three stages of family development, whereas for mothers, their couple relationship satisfaction was not relevant until the oldest child reached adolescence. This can be understood as evidence for the fathering vulnerability hypothesis (Cummings et al., 2010). Supporting data from Bouchard and Lee (2000), parenthood is more strongly embedded in the coparent relationship and familial framework conditions for fathers than for mothers. We found that mothers' couple relationship satisfaction becomes relevant for their satisfaction with paternal behaviour when the children reach adolescence. In contrast, their ratings of the father's willingness to spend time with the child become irrelevant at that time. We interpret this shift in focus to couple relationship characteristics as an indicator that the adjustment to the prospective empty nest situation has begun. As Seiffge-Krenke (2009) states, children gradually spend less time with their parents, especially with their fathers, when they reach adolescence. Therefore, mothers with an oldest child in adolescence can no longer rely on the father's willingness to spend time with the child when evaluating fatherhood and instead take into account their couple relationship satisfaction.

In addition, fathers' underestimation of mothers' satisfaction with paternal behaviour may be an indicator that fathers' hold an elementary uncertainty about the fathering role, which, to some extent may be rooted in maternal gatekeeping processes and to some extent may be rooted in the lack of adequate male parenting role models (Daly et al., 2009) or the increasing diversity of fatherhood (e.g., van Dongen, Frinking, & Jacobs, 1995).

In sum, our results imply that research on fatherhood, in principle, need not be restricted to fathers' perspectives but should include mothers' perspectives too. Thereby, the conceptualization of what a good father is like from fathers' as well as mothers' points of view can help researchers to reveal negotiation processes within couples. The consideration of different stages of family development is an additional demand for fatherhood research because, as shown in the present study, mothers' evaluations of fatherhood are based on different aspects as the family develops.

Some limitations of this study should also be noted. First, certain variables are single-item measures whose statistical quality is probably not optimal. However, couple relationship satisfaction is thought to be adequately captured by a single-item measure as Noyon and Kock (2006) have demonstrated. Nevertheless, the single-item measure of mothers' and fathers' views on mothers' satisfaction with paternal behaviour remains deficient. Second, the present study relied solely on the questionnaire method, thus bearing the risk of social desirability and other biases. Third, the independent variables that we applied represent a limited selection. Rather distal (e.g., social support) or proximal (e.g., personality traits) predictors were not included even though they may be notably relevant. Fourth, the regression coefficients may have been inflated due to the fact that most of them represent relations between variables that were surveyed by single informants. Fifth, some of the bivariate correlations between the predictor variables were quite strong and may therefore indicate collinearity. Sixth, the cross-sectional design of the present study prohibits causal interpretations.

Despite these limitations, the present study has some advantages and contributes to the research on fatherhood in a novel way. To our knowledge, this is the first study to simultaneously include an external perspective on fatherhood as well as the father's point of view on this external perspective on fatherhood. In combination with data on possible predictors of these evaluations of fatherhood from fathers' as well as mothers' points of view, the present study is able to provide deeper insight into mothers' and fathers' different perspectives on fatherhood. It thereby reveals differences between the self- and external ratings of mothers' satisfaction with paternal behaviour, thus suggesting that fathers underestimate their partners' satisfaction. Possible topics of couples' negotiations were detected via the disclosure of the different origination of fathers' versus mothers' views on mothers' satisfaction with paternal behaviour. The inclusion of couples from different stages of family development and the fact that these stages are tightly defined by the age of the oldest child in the family are additional advantages of the study design, and this study design puts forth a first peak into how mothers' satisfaction with paternal behaviour may change across the family life cycle.

REFERENCES

Bonney, J. F., Kelly, M. L., & Levant, R. F. (1999). A model of fathers' behavioral involvement in child care in dual-earner families. *Journal of Family Psychology, 13*, 401–415. doi:10.1037/0893-3200.13.3.401

Bouchard, G., & Lee, C. M. (2000). The marital context for father involvement with their preschool children. The role of partner support. *Journal of Prevention, 10*, 37–53.

Brown, G. L., Mangelsdorf, S. C., & Neff, C. (2012). Father involvement, paternal sensitivity, and father–child attachment security in the first 3 years. *Journal of Family Psychology, 26*, 421–430.

Cannon, E. A., Schoppe-Sullivan, S. J., Mangelsdorf, S. C., Brown, G. L., & Szewczyk Sokolowski, M. (2008). Parent characteristics as antecedents of maternal gatekeeping and fathering behavior. *Family Process, 47*, 501–519. doi:10.1111/j.1545-5300.2008.00268.x

Cowan, C. P., & Cowan, P. A. (1987). Men's involvement in parenthood. Identifying the antecedents and understanding the barriers. In P. W. Berman & F. A. Pedersen (Eds.), *Men's transitions to parenthood. Longitudinal studies of early family experience* (pp. 145–174). Hillsdale, NJ: Lawrence Erlbaum.

Cummings, E. M., Merrilees, C. E., & George, M. (2010). Fathers, marriages, and families: Revisiting and updating the framework for fathering in family context. In M. E. Lamb (Ed.), *The role of the father in child development* (pp. 154–176). Hoboken, NJ: John Wiley & Sons.

Daly, K. J., Ashbourne, L., & Brown, J. L. (2009). Fathers' perceptions of children's influence: Implications for involvement. *The Annals of the American Academy of Political and Social Science, 624*, 61–77. doi:10.1177/0002716209334695

DeLuccie, M. F. (1995). Mothers as gatekeepers: A model of maternal mediators of father involvement. *The Journal of Genetic Psychology, 156*, 115–131. Retrieved from Psychology and Behavioral Sciences Collection Database (Accession Number: 9505051888).

Erel, O., & Burman, B. (1995). Interrelatedness of marital relations and parent–child relations: A meta-analytic review. *Psychological Bulletin, 118*, 108–132. doi:10.1037/0033-2909.118.1.108

Fagan, J., & Barnett, M. (2003). The relationship between maternal gatekeeping, paternal competence, mothers' attitudes about the father role, and father involvement. *Journal of Family Issues, 24*, 1020–1043. doi:10.1177/0192513X03256397

Field, A. (2009). *Discovering statistics using SPSS*. London: Sage.

Fuhrmans, F., von der Lippe, H., & Fuhrer, U. (2012). Subjektive Vaterschaftskonzepte. Eine empirische Studie zu Vätern und ihren Partnerinnen [Subjective views on fatherhood. An empirical study of fathers and their partners]. In H. Walter & A. Eickhorst (Eds.), *Das Väter-Handbuch. Theorie, Forschung, Praxis* [The handbook of fathers. Theories, research, practice] (pp. 299–323). Gießen: Psychosozial.

Krishnakumar, A., & Black, M. M. (2003). Family process within three-generation households and adolescent mothers' satisfaction with father involvement. *Journal of Family Psychology, 17*, 488–498. doi:10.1037/0893-3200.17.4.488

Kulik, L., & Tsoref, H. (2010). The entrance in the maternal garden. Environmental and personal variables that explain maternal gatekeeping. *Journal of Gender Studies, 19*, 263–277. doi:10.1080/09589236.2010.494342

Matzner, M. (2004). *Vaterschaft aus der Sicht von Vätern* [Fatherhood from the perspective of fathers]. Wiesbaden: VS.

McBride, B. A., Brown, G. L., Bost, K. K., Shin, N., Vaughn, B., & Korth, B. (2005). Paternal identity, maternal gatekeeping, and father involvment. *Family Relations, 54*, 360–372.

Noyon, A., & Kock, T. (2006). Living apart together. Ein Vergleich getrennt wohnender Paare mit klassischen Partnerschaften [Couples living apart compared with couples in traditional living arrangements]. *Zeitschrift für Familienforschung* [Journal of Family Research], *18*, 27–45.

Palkovitz, R. J. (2002). *Involved fathering and men's adult development. Provisional balances.* Mahwah, NJ: Lawrence Erlbaum.

Pedro, M. F., Ribeiro, T., & Shelton, K. H. (2012). Marital satisfaction and partners' parenting practices: The mediating role of coparenting behavior. *Journal of Family Psychology, 26,* 509–522. doi:10.1037/a0029121

Schoppe-Sullivan, S. J., Brown, G. L., Cannon, E. A., Mangelsdorf, S. C., & Szewczyk Sokolowski, M. (2008). Maternal gatekeeping, coparenting quality, and fathering behavior in families with infants. *Journal of Family Psychology, 22,* 389–398. doi:10.1037/0893-3200.22.3.389

Seiffge-Krenke, I. (2009). *Psychotherapie und Entwicklungspsychologie: Beziehungen: Herausforderungen, Ressourcen, Risiken* [Psychotherapy and developmental psychology: Relations, challenges, resources, risks]. Heidelberg: Springer.

Simmerman, S., Blacher, J., & Baker, B. L. (2001). Fathers' and mothers' perceptions of father involvement in families with young children with a disability. *Journal of Intellectual and Developmental Disability, 26,* 325–338. doi:10.1080/13668250120087335

Tremblay, S., & Pierce, T. (2011). Perceptions of fatherhood: Longitudinal reciprocal associations within the couple. *Canadian Journal of Behavioural Science, 43,* 99–110. doi:10.1037/a0022635

Van Dongen, M., Frinking, G., & Jacobs, M. (Eds.). (1995). *Changing fatherhood: A multidisciplinary perspective.* Amsterdam: Thesis Publishers.

Wenger-Schittenhelm, H., & Walter, H. (2002). Das Konstanzer Väterinstrument: Ein Fragebogen zu erlebter Vaterschaft [The Constance Father Inventory. A questionnaire on the experience of fatherhood]. In H. Walter (Ed.), *Männer als Väter. Sozialwissenschaftliche Theorie und Empirie* [Human males as fathers. Social science theory and empirical results] (pp. 419–454). Gießen: Psychosozial.

Paternal involvement elevates trajectories of life satisfaction during transition to parenthood

Alexandru Agache[1], Birgit Leyendecker[1],
Esther Schäfermeier[2], and Axel Schölmerich[1]

[1]Department of Developmental Psychology, Ruhr-Universität Bochum, Bochum, Germany
[2]Zentrum für Diagnostik und Förderung, University of Cologne, Cologne, Germany

This study explored the role of fathers' involvement for life satisfaction changes among 598 cohabitating couples before and after childbirth using data from the German Socio-Economic Panel (GSOEP). We included longitudinal data and reports from both parents on their time spent on housework and childcare and their life satisfaction. Piecewise latent growth models showed that fathers' relative involvement trajectories for housework and childcare (amount of time men spent compared to their partners) were positively correlated. Fathers' relative involvement was perceived as supportive for mothers' childcare. In families where fathers were more involved, life satisfaction trajectories were much steeper; both parents had elevated levels around birth and returned to their baseline levels compared to families with less-involved fathers. Fathers who were less involved did not increase in life satisfaction at birth and decreased below their baseline levels within the third year post-birth.

According to worldwide surveys, people perceive childbirth as a desirable and positive life event (e.g., Vanassche, Swicegood, & Matthijs, 2013), but findings on the benefits of parenthood for well-being are mixed; childbirth brings more "joy than misery" (Nelson, Kushlev, English, Dunn, & Lyubomirsky, 2013) and becoming a parent is both detrimental and rewarding (Nomaguchi & Milkie, 2003). Parenthood appears to be associated with decreased well-being as measured by life-satisfaction scales (Hansen, 2012). In the results from a recent meta-analysis by Luhmann, Hofmann, Eid, and Lucas (2012), parents'

131

trajectories bear some similarities with the flight of Icarus: the birth of the first child gives people wings to fly high, but this positive effect starts to melt after childbirth, and within two years life satisfaction decreases below the original baseline levels.

Few longitudinal studies examined the role of fathers' involvement on both parents' transitions into parenthood. They identified positive links between fathers' involvement during pregnancy and maternal health outcomes (Redshaw & Henderson, 2013), and paternal childcare and relationship quality (Schober, 2012). There is also evidence for the positive association between prenatal and postnatal paternal involvement (Cabrera, Fagan, & Farrie, 2008; Cook, Jones, Dick, & Singh, 2005).

A major aim of our paper was to determine whether paternal involvement is reflected in higher levels of parents' life satisfaction before, around, and after childbirth.

CHILDBIRTH AND LIFE-SATISFACTION TRAJECTORIES

According to the set-point theory, life-satisfaction levels are stable and life events cause only short-term fluctuations that eventually return to initial levels (for a review, see Diener, Lucas, & Scollon, 2006). Lucas and colleagues suggested that some life events (e.g., divorce, unemployment or disability) have long-lasting negative effects (Lucas, 2007).

Few longitudinal studies examined life-satisfaction trajectories in the years surrounding childbirth. These studies found initial life-satisfaction increases during pregnancy, which peaked at the time of birth, then decreased and returned to the baseline or below (Germany: Clark, Diener, Georgellis, & Lucas, 2008; Germany and UK: Myrskylä & Margolis, 2012; Australia: Frijters, Johnston, & Shields, 2011). More recently, Dyrdal and Lucas (2013), using GSOEP data and hierarchical modelling, found a negative net effect after adjusting for changes in partnership status.

Research addressing what factors influence parents' reactions and adaptations to parenthood is both scarce and inconclusive. For example, Myrskylä and Margolis (2012) found a positive, long-term effect of mothers' age and socioeconomic status on post-birth trajectories. However, Dyrdal and Lucas (2013) found no effect of income, yet a small effect of personality factor and additional births and a long-term positive effect of age. How parents support each other in raising children has not been addressed.

PATERNAL INVOLVEMENT AND SUPPORT IN CHILDCARE

Several theories have been formulated on paternal involvement mostly focusing on fathers' direct interactions with their children (Cabrera, Fitzgerald, Bradley, & Roggman, 2007). Lamb, Pleck, Charnov, and Levine (1985) first introduced the concept of fathers' involvement and proposed fathers' interactions as a prominent involvement dimension. Empirical studies distinguished between multidimensional aspects of fathers' involvement (Pleck, 2010), but the amount of time fathers spend with their children remained central (e.g., Wical & Doherty, 2005). There is little evidence that the absolute time of father-child interactions has a direct effect on parents' life satisfaction. Although fathers tend to feel more strained for time with their children, only mothers' life satisfaction was affected when they reported feeling strained for time with their children (Nomaguchi, Milkie, & Bianchi, 2005).

Fathers who spend more time with their children are more likely to be supportive in social interactions (Almeida, Wethington, & McDonald, 2001). They also may benefit in life satisfaction because of an increase in family interactions (Knoester & Eggebeen, 2006). Fathers not only influence themselves and their children by these interactions, but their involvement is also strongly tied to mothers' well-being and marital satisfaction (see Cummings, Merrilees, & George, 2010).

While only few longitudinal studies have investigated the positive link between parental well-being and fathers' involvement in childcare (e.g., Riina & Feinberg, 2012), division of housework during transition to parenthood has received less attention. Childbirth brings the most powerful shift in time allocation; mothers become the main caregivers and are mainly responsible for housework, while fathers increase their work hours. This general pattern has recently been documented in several countries using nationally representative time-use data (Germany: Kühhirt, 2012; USA: Bianchi, Sayer, Milkie, & Robinson, 2012). A cross-sectional analysis with representative samples from 23 European countries found negative consequences for maternal happiness when the share of housework for women was greater than 75% (Mencarini & Sironi, 2012). Few studies include fathers' involvement in both childcare and housework, and findings are mixed, pointing to differential effects on parents' well-being. Fathers' lack of involvement in childcare, but not housework, was negatively linked to distress in mothers (e.g., Goldberg & Perry-Jenkins, 2004).

Family systems theory stresses the notion of interdependent support between mothers and fathers' involvement as a basis for mutual, supportive, co-parental relationships (Cox, Paley, & Harter, 2001). Findings indicated that fathers' involvement is a predictor for co-parenting behaviours (Fagan & Cabrera, 2012) with children as the main beneficiaries (Palkovitz, Fagan, & Hull, 2012); however, we can assume that shared responsibility of child rearing and joint division of household tasks also contributes to mothers' well-being (Nomaguchi, Brown, & Leyman, 2012). Therefore, we expected that higher shares of fathers' time spent on childcare and housework would be perceived by mothers as supportive, and would positively influence mothers' and fathers' life satisfaction.

RESEARCH QUESTIONS

Using GSOEP study data, we investigated if paternal involvement is associated with higher life satisfaction during the transition into parenthood, as measured at three annual waves before and after childbirth. We defined transition into parenthood as a positive developmental phase if both parents' life-satisfaction levels were elevated by childbirth and did not decline below baseline levels within three years after childbirth. We limited the post-birth period to a maximum of three years because, in Germany, children typically enter childcare at this time, which may be a new demanding phase for parents. We used longitudinal time-use reports for mothers and fathers on housework and childcare, and one maternal subjective measure of fathers' support in childcare.

Based on the family systemic view, we expected that mothers would perceive fathers' time spent on childcare and housework as supportive. Specifically, we expected that higher paternal involvement would be associated with a steeper increase in both mothers' and fathers' life satisfaction around the time of birth of the first child, and not decline beyond the original baseline in the years following birth. Conversely, we expected that lower levels of paternal involvement would be associated with lower life-satisfaction levels.

METHODS

We used data from the GSOEP, a nationally representative longitudinal annual panel study of private households and individuals (details in Wagner, Frick, & Schupp, 2007). Because mothers' ratings of fathers' support in childcare were collected only starting with 2003, we selected only healthy first-born children born between 2003 and 2009 living with both biological parents, resulting in a total sample of 1196 men and women ($N = 598$ couples). Parents' relationship duration before childbirth averaged 41.39 months; 67% of parents were married and 100% were living within the same household at the year of birth and did not separate or divorce within the three years after birth. Data were selected before and after birth from six annual waves: T1: ~2.6 years pre-birth; T2: ~1.6 years pre-birth; T3: ~0.6 years pre-birth; T4: ~6 months following birth; T5: ~1.6 years post-birth; and T6: ~2.6 years post-birth.

Measures

Life satisfaction. Life satisfaction was assessed annually using an 11-point scale with the question: "How satisfied are you at present with your life as a whole?". Answers ranged from 0 (*totally dissatisfied*) to 10 (*totally satisfied*). The variance of the measure was considerable (see Table 1). Mean values for men and women were high across all waves (e.g., within the months post-birth: $M = 7.77$ [$SD = 1.46$] for women; $M = 7.41$ [$SD = 1.48$] for men.

TABLE 1

Means (and standard deviations) of mothers' and fathers' life satisfaction and their weekday hours in housework and childcare across all measurement points (years and months before and after the birth of the first child)

	T1 (−2.6 Years)	T2 (−1.6 Years)	T3 (−6 Months)	T4 (+6 Months)	T5 (+1.6 Years)	T6 (+2.6 Years)
Fathers' life satisfaction	7.29	7.23	7.41	7.41	7.13	7.10
	(1.31)	(1.40)	(1.51)	(1.48)	(1.50)	(1.54)
Mothers' life satisfaction	7.43	7.44	7.72	7.77	7.37	7.44
	(1.47)	(1.41)	(1.38)	(1.46)	(1.56)	(1.44)
Fathers' hours in housework	0.91	0.86	0.87	0.80	0.84	0.82
	(0.82)	(0.74)	(0.75)	(0.82)	(0.84)	(0.86)
Mothers' hours in housework	1.47	1.51	1.69	2.87	2.77	2.69
	(0.97)	(1.01)	(1.08)	(1.67)	(1.59)	(1.55)
Fathers' hours in childcare				2.37	2.61	2.60
				(3.06)	(2.61)	(2.78)
Mothers' hours in childcare				11.88	10.40	10.18
				(6.29)	(6.27)	(6.22)

Time spent with housework and childcare. Both spouses reported their typical hours spent on housework and childcare in one workday. The raw values of the measures are presented in Table 1. To examine trajectories of fathers' relative involvement in housework and childcare, men's hours within each dyad were multiplied by 100 and then divided by the spouses' reported hours. The resulting proportional scores reflected men's relative amounts of time use compared to their spouses (i.e., 0 indicated no sharing, whereas 100 indicated equal sharing).

Support in childcare. Mothers rated fathers' supportiveness in childcare when children were approximately six months old on a four-point scale (1 = *not supported*, 2 = *less supported*, 3 = *somehow supported* and 4 = *very supported*). Ratings were grouped into three categories: (1) "unsupportive", based on the first two answer categories of *no support* (n = 2) and *less supported* (n = 99); (2) "medium supportive" (so-named because it was also the median of the measure), based on the answer category of *somehow supported* (n = 264); (3) "highly supportive", based on the fourth answer category of *very supported* (n = 234).

Socio-demographics and additional controls. At each wave, each couple member reported their working hours per day. As a proxy for unemployment, we calculated each parent's cumulative unemployment history from all months before the child was around six months old.

We dichotomized each parent's education degree into either below lower-secondary degree (ISCED I-II coded with 0) or above upper-secondary degree (coded with 1).

We selected annual net disposable household income assessed for the year before childbirth as a proxy for families' material resources during the pregnancy and the first months after birth. Income data were transformed using the new OECD equivalence scale, which weighs for age and number of household members.

Additional measures included parents' age at their first child's birth, the degree of pregnancy planning (maternal ratings: 0 = *rather not planned*; 1 = *rather planned*), birth cohorts and mothers' additional births. Birth cohorts were dichotomized into births before or after the year 2007, when a new law on parental leave was introduced in Germany.

Analytic strategy

We first compared fathers' share in housework and childcare across the three groups of supportive fathers (repeated-measures ANOVAs conducted with IBM SPSS 21). Parents' life-satisfaction trajectories and fathers' shares of housework and childcare were then analyzed with the piecewise latent growth models (Duncan, Duncan, & Strycker, 2006, Chapter 9) depicted in Figure 1. Because we expected higher variability due to childbirth, we specified a linear rate of change across the three waves preceding birth and a linear change rate for the three post-birth waves.

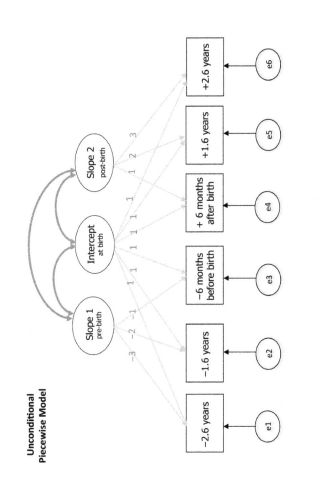

Figure 1. Latent growth analysis model.

The latent growth variables mean represented the average trend of change across all individual slopes and intercepts of mothers or fathers while allowing each individual in the sample to have its own trajectory. Growth factors variance represented the interindividual variability around these trends. Since childbirth occurred between the third and fourth measurement wave, the loadings of the slope coefficients were fixed at [-3-2-1000] for the first pre-birth slope and [000123] for the post-birth slope such that the intercept for both slopes was centred where the zero loadings overlapped between the third and fourth wave (see Figure 1). To control for dyadic dependencies, we correlated the errors of the life-satisfaction measures between mothers and fathers (Kenny, Kashy, & Cook, 2006).

Using multigroup analysis, we investigated whether parents' life-satisfaction trajectories differed across the couples with unsupportive, medium, and highly supportive fathers in childcare. This allowed a comparison between the intercept and rates of change across groups and to test for differences in the model-based estimated means at each time point (i.e., baseline and endline). To calculate effect sizes of the differences between two estimated means, we used Cohen's *d* formula (Cohen, 1988) and divided the sum of the two means by the square root mean of their variances.

To address missing data in ANOVAs, we used single-use data imputation based on the expectation-maximization algorithm that performs best when conducting descriptive analyses (Enders, 2010). Inspection of the correlations before and after imputation yielded no significant differences. To manage missing data when analyzing latent growth we used Bayesian model estimation as implemented in Mplus 7 (Muthén & Muthén, 1998–2012). With Bayesian estimation, covariances are fitted into the model covariance structure and into each participant based on all available data and without data imputation (for technical details see Asparouhov & Muthén, 2010). We chose Bayes estimation (with non-informative priors) because it is highly accurate in the estimation of latent models with a high number of parameters (Muthén & Asparouhov, 2012). All latent growth models were analyzed with the Mplus program (scripts can be obtained from the first author). All estimated means were depicted using the R-package ggplot2 (Wickham, 2009).

RESULTS

Fathers' involvement, support in childcare, and sociodemographics

We explored whether fathers' relative involvement measures were associated with mothers' ratings of support in childcare. We compared fathers' trajectories of shares in housework and childcare across groups with low (LS), medium (MS) and highly supportive (HS) fathers using ANOVAs with repeated measures and controlling for sociodemographics. Because fathers' shares were assessed for a typical workday, we included both parents' working hours in the preliminary analysis (see Figure 2). Except for fathers' workings hours, a significant change existed before and after childbirth in all trajectories.

Fathers' shares in housework gradually decreased before birth (see Figure 2a). Supportive fathers shared between 60%–80% of the housework before childbirth compared to 50% of LS-fathers [F (2, 586) = 8.97, $p < .001$, $\eta^2 = .03$]; the MS/HS-men shared more than $\sim 40\%$ compared to LS-men (~ 24 to $\sim 31\%$) in the three post-birth years. The decline in fathers' shares in housework around birth reflects an increase in spouses' housework hours (separate analyses for each measurement point showed no significant differences in women's housework hours across the three groups).

On average, differences in childcare trajectories were more evident compared to housework (see Figure 2b). HS-men increased their shares from $\sim 33\%$ to $\sim 47\%$ within the first three years compared to LS-men (shares from $\sim 18\%$ to $\sim 28\%$); simple between-contrasts: F (2, 584) = 4.97, $p < .01$, $\eta^2 = .02$. Separate ANOVAS for each time point revealed that HS-fathers had higher shares in childcare at the first two post-birth waves compared to MS-fathers; at six months: F (2, 595) = 8.26, $p < .01$, $\eta^2 = .03$; at 1.6 years: F (2, 595) = 5.27, $p < .01$, $\eta^2 = .02$.

To sum up, fathers of first-borns were perceived as highly supportive by their spouses if they shared more than $\sim 60\%$ in housework before birth and more than $\sim 40\%$ (housework) and $\sim 35\%$ (childcare) right after birth.

Mothers from the HS-group had slightly higher working hours in the second year after birth; the between-effect was not significant (see Figure 2c). A significant between-effect existed for men's working hours (see Figure 2d). LS-men reported more working hours than supportive men across all time points; simple contrasts: F (2, 586) = 7.34 $p < .001$, $\eta^2 = .02$. MS/HS-fathers did not differ in working hours.

Parents from the MS/HS-groups were older at childbirth and mothers from the LS-group had a longer unemployment history at birth (see Table 2); these differences were small (0–1% in explained variance). A multivariate probit-regression with all sociodemographics as predictors and support in childcare as the dependent variable revealed that mothers' unemployment history had a marginal effect ($z = -.11$, $p < .10$). Because of these small effects, we excluded sociodemographics from further analysis.

Life satisfaction and fathers' relative involvement

As expected, parents' life satisfaction increased before childbirth (positive slope parameter), maxed at birth, and decreased. The slopes at post-birth were larger than pre-birth; after childbirth life satisfaction decreased more rapidly compared to increases seen before birth. Life satisfaction was higher and increased more

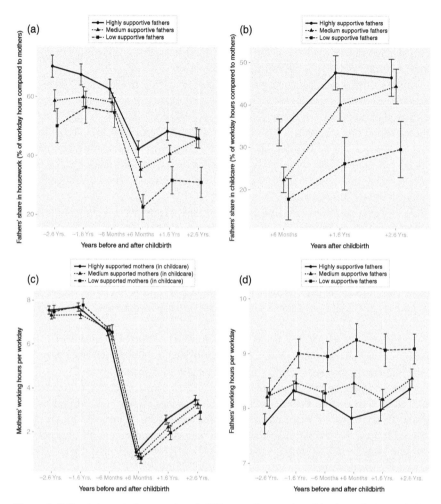

Figure 2. Fathers' shares in housework and childcare and parents' working hours before and after childbirth across the groups of low, medium and highly supportive fathers in childcare. *Note:* Estimated means with *SE* (error bars) adjusted for sociodemographics, degree of pregnancy planning and additional births (unemployment history was excluded as a covariate when analyzing parents' working hours).

intensively around birth for mothers compared to fathers. Only men decreased in satisfaction below the baseline levels three years after birth ($d = .20$).

Correlations between the life satisfaction pre-birth slope and intercept at birth were positive; those who increased more in life satisfaction had higher levels of satisfaction around birth. The negative correlation between the pre- and post-birth slope simply reflects that parents who increased life satisfaction around

TABLE 2

Differences in sociodemographics across couples with low, medium and highly supportive fathers in childcare

		Low supportive fathers (LS) (n = 101)	Medium supportive fathers (MS) (n = 263)	Highly supportive fathers (HS) (n = 234)	F	Partial η^2
Mothers' age at birth (years)	M	28.54[a]	29.30[ab]	30.20[b]	4.11*	.014
	(SD)	(5.03)	(5.21)	(5.16)		
Fathers' age at birth (years)	M	31.87[a]	32.41[ab]	33.64[b]	3.97*	.013
	(SD)	(5.58)	(5.99)	(6.30)		
Annual family net (equivalized) income during the pre-birth year	M	17717.28	18902.68	20081.03	2.78	.009
	(SD)	(7578.27)	(8412.23)	(9538.58)		
Mothers' unemployment history (months until birth)	M	0.61[a]	0.34[b]	0.36[b]	3.50*	.012
	(SD)	(1.16)	(0.76)	(0.95)		
Fathers' unemployment history (months until birth)	M	0.61	0.73	0.68	0.31	.001
	(SD)	(0.99)	(1.33)	(1.37)		
Mothers' higher education (> ISCED 2)	%	47.5	44.5	50.4		
Fathers' higher education (> ISCED 2)	%	38.6	45.2	43.2		
Birth cohort 2007	%	33.7	37.3	34.6		
Planned births	%	73.3	75.3	75.6		
Additional births (1 year after first birth)	%	4.0	4.6	3.8		
Additional births (2 years after first birth)	%	13.9	12.9	14.5		

Notes: * $p < .05$. [ab] Numbers with different letter superscript differ significantly across groups (ANOVAs with Sidak post-hoc tests); Bonferroni z-tests were used for testing differences between percentages across groups, but no significant differences were found.

birth had higher decreases after birth. Consistent with GSOEP results (Dyrdal & Lucas, 2013), changes were similar across mothers and fathers within the same couple (.98 and .75 for pre- and post-birth, respectively).

Concerning fathers' relative involvement, changes estimated in the growth model were consistent with ANOVA results; before birth a systematic decline in fathers' relative participation in housework emerged (see Table 3). Fathers' participation in childcare yielded an overall positive trend after birth.

Fathers' shares in housework and childcare correlated positively (see Table 3). The pre-birth slope in housework and mothers' life satisfaction at birth yielded a medium positive correlation. All other correlations involving life-satisfaction were not significant.

Support in childcare as moderator for life-satisfaction trajectories

Results of the multi-group analysis comparing the trajectories of parents' life satisfaction across mothers' ratings of fathers' support in childcare are presented in Table 4. The Bayesian model fit was good with the lower bounds of the 95% - χ^2-credible interval below 0 and the posterior probability greater than .05 (see Table 4).

The covariances between all growth factors were freely estimated across groups; no significant differences between groups were found (results not shown). The means and variances of change factors for both spouses from couples with MS/HS-men were significant (see Figure 3; estimated means based on model parameters reported in Table 4).

Mothers and fathers from the LS-group had the lowest levels of life satisfaction and did not change before and after childbirth (shown by non-significant slopes). Although the difference between spouses in this group was small at baseline, a marginal effect emerged in the third year after birth (10% significance); about 55% of LS-fathers became less satisfied compared to their spouses ($d = .20$).

Mothers from the HS-group had significantly higher life satisfaction at birth than did LS-mothers ($d = .69$). Because the 95% credible interval [.33; 1.06] did not contain zero, this result was significant (credible interval is the Bayesian equivalent of confidence interval).

It is important to note that the differences in both parents' trajectories across groups were gradual: LS $<$ MS $<$ HS. Mothers from the HS-group differ at baseline only slightly from MS-mothers ($d = .10$). At birth, differences between these two groups of supported mothers double in size ($d = .24$). This effect is significant because it means that $\sim 30\%$ of the HS-mothers gain more at birth in life satisfaction than MS-mothers.

HS-fathers life satisfaction at birth compared to MS/LS-fathers almost doubled (i.e., $d = .27$ at baseline and $d = .52$ at birth). While all mothers returned

TABLE 3

Means, variances and factor correlations from the pricewise growth models of parents' life satisfaction and fathers' relative involvement in housework and childcare

	Means	Variances	1	2	3	4	5	6	7	8	9	10
1. Intercept (birth), life satisfaction, mothers	7.87*	1.98*	1									
2. Pre-birth Slope 1, life satisfaction, mothers	.17*	.12*	.27	1								
3. Post-birth Slope 2, life satisfaction, mothers	−.17*	.07*	−.10	−.43*	1							
4. Intercept (birth), life satisfaction, fathers	7.51*	1.80*	.73*	.41*	−.22	1						
5. Pre-birth Slope 1, life satisfaction, fathers	.09*	.13*	.39*	.98*	−.40†	.53*	1					
6. Post-birth Slope 2, life satisfaction, fathers	−.14*	.18*	−.19	−.51*	.75*	−.39*	−.55*	1				
7. Intercept (birth), fathers' involvement in housework	38.07*	627.66*	.17	.05	.05	.11	.23	.04	1			
8. Pre-birth Slope 1, fathers' involvement in housework	−10.63*	223.46*	.31†	.28	−.14	.23	.17	−.32	.27	1		
9. Post-birth Slope 2, fathers' involvement in housework	1.07	115.16*	−.43	.02	−.28	−.29	−.59	−.08	.16	−.29	1	
10. Intercept (6 months after birth), fathers' involvement in childcare	26.35*	242.84*	−.09	−.06	.15	−.01	−.03	−.07	.44*	.11	−.07	1
11. Post-birth Slope, fathers' involvement in childcare	7.59*	166.52*	.01	.02	−.16	−.07	−.10	.00	.10	.27*	.74*	−.43*

Bayesian model fit (unconditional piecewise growth models)

Mothers' and fathers' life satisfaction: 95% CI for the difference between observed and replicated χ^2 values = −16.06, 55.72, posterior predictive p-value = .14
Fathers' involvement in housework: 95% CI for the difference between observed and replicated χ^2 values = −6.581, 44.85, posterior predictive p-value = .06
Fathers' involvement in childcare: 95% CI for the difference between observed and replicated χ^2 values = 46.72, 83.33, posterior predictive p-value = .000

Notes: $^*p < .05$, $^†p < .10$. Means and variances resulted from three separate, unconditional models: on parents' life satisfaction, and on fathers' relative involvement in housework and childcare. Correlations were estimated pairwise by including in separate models only two trajectories (i.e., only mothers' life satisfaction and fathers' involvement in childcare). For estimating the correlations involving fathers' shares in childcare time was centred at six months after birth (the first available measurement for childcare).

TABLE 4

Trajectories in life satisfaction across the couples with low supportive (LS), medium supportive (MS), and highly supportive (HS) fathers in childcare

	Means			d-Effect Sizes for Mean Differences [95% Credible Interval]					
	LS	MS	HS	HS > LS	MS > LS	HS > MS	Within LS	Within MS	Within HS
Mothers									
Baseline (2.6 Yrs. before birth)	7.16*	7.34*	7.50*	.19 [−.06, .43]	.01 [−.15, .34]	.10 [−.09, .29]	—	—	—
Intercept (at birth)	7.24*	7.88*	8.14*	.69* [.33, 1.06]	.48* [.14, .84]	.24† [−.02, .51]	—	—	—
Endline (2.6 Yrs. after birth)	7.13*	7.31*	7.52*	.24* [.01, .48]	.11 [−.12, .34]	.13 [−.05, .31]	—	—	—
Baseline > Endline	—	—	—				.01 [−.19, .21]	.01 [−.10, .14]	−.01 [−.16, .14]
Slope 1 (pre-birth)	.03	.18*	.21*						
Slope 2 (post-birth)	−.04	−.19*	−.21*						
Fathers									
Baseline (2.6 Yrs. before birth)	6.86*	7.30*	7.35*	.27* [.02, .55]	.27† [−.01, .54]	.04 [−.16, .22]			
Intercept (at birth)	7.05*	7.40*	7.86*	.52* [.19, .87]	.21 [−.11, .53]	.35* [.11, .60]			
Endline (2.6 Yrs. after birth)	6.80*	6.99*	7.32*	.30* [.04, .55]	.11 [−.14, .36]	.20* [.01, .38]			
Baseline > Endline	—	—	—				.03 [−.24, .30]	.20* [.05, .34]	.02 [−.11, .16]
Slope 1 (pre-birth)	.06	.03	.17*						
Slope 2 (post-birth)	−.08	−.13*	−.18*						
Mothers > Fathers									
Baseline (2.6 Yrs. before birth)	—	—	—	—	—	—	.16 [−.08, .40]	.03 [−.13, .18]	.09 [−.07, .24]
Intercept (at birth)	—	—	—	—	—	—	.12 [−.19, .41]	.39* [.19, .59]	.25* [.06, .45]
Endline (2.6 Yrs. after birth)	—	—	—	—	—	—	.19† [−.05, .43]	.19* [.06, .33]	.12† [−.01, .25]

Notes: *p < .05, †p < .10. Bayesian model fit (multigroup piecewise latent growth model): 95% CI for the difference between observed and replicated χ^2 values = −24.63, 106.21 posterior predictive *p*- value = .10.

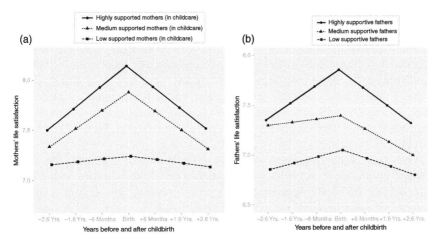

Figure 3. Life satisfaction trajectories across couples with low, medium and highly supportive fathers in childcare. *Note:* Estimated means from the multigroup dyadic piecewise growth model (Bayesian estimation).

to baseline levels within three years after birth, only HS-fathers returned. MS-fathers' increase at birth was similar to LS-fathers, small and not significant; at birth, satisfaction was not significantly higher compared to LS-fathers. The third year after birth ∼55% of MS-fathers dropped below baseline ($d = .20$).

To sum up, only supported mothers and highly supportive fathers increased life satisfaction at birth and gradually returned to baseline levels after birth.

DISCUSSION

This is the first study to document variations in childbirth effects on parents' life satisfaction by levels of paternal involvement. We addressed this gap in the literature by using longitudinal data from the GSOEP study. Overall, our results are consistent with previous research (Dyrdal & Lucas, 2013) that life satisfaction was likely to peak around the actual birth of the first child, followed by a decline to or below baseline levels. However, consistent with our expectation, life satisfaction of both parents was contingent on fathers' involvement. We found that trajectories of fathers' relative involvement in housework and childcare (amount of time men spent compared to their partners) were positively correlated. Moreover, fathers' relative involvement in both childcare and housework was perceived as supportive for mothers' childcare. We also demonstrated that fathers' support in childcare was associated with higher levels of life satisfaction in both parents in the years surrounding childbirth. These findings add to the growing literature concerning fathers' instrumental involvement as emotional resources for mothers (e.g., Nomaguchi et al., 2012), and suggest that fathers' involvement is a resource for their own well-being.

Our major finding concerns the role of paternal involvement for variability in both mothers' and fathers' life satisfaction. While mothers' life-satisfaction levels returned to baseline within ~2.6 years post-birth, only the highly supportive fathers followed this pattern. In contrast, the trajectories of fathers with medium levels of involvement and support were less steep and dropped below baseline levels within ~2.6 years post-birth. The accelerated trajectory decline of fathers with lower involvement suggests that fathers' involvement has long-term positive effects for their life satisfaction (see also Riina & Feinberg, 2012).

Our main findings suggest pathways of bidirectional influences between fathers' involvement and mothers' life satisfaction, which is in line with recent articulations of family systems theories (for a review, see Holmes, Cowan, Cowan, & Hawkins, 2012). Both parents seem to profit from fathers' involvement. A possible interpretation of this finding is that fathers' involvement might be directly linked to relationship quality. Several studies have shown a similar drop in relationship quality during the first two years after childbirth (e.g., Doss, Rhoades, Stanley, & Markman, 2009). During this time, the couple has to figure out new ways of partnership and they might quarrel over routine problems and division of labour at home. High father involvement might buffer potential risks for marital conflicts, while low involvement might lead to or result from these conflicts. Fathers with an increased vulnerability in marital conflicts might also withdraw from interactions with their children as they lack clearly defined roles as parents compared to mothers (e.g., Cummings, Merrilees, & George, 2012).

Finally, our results do not indicate long-term positive effects of childbirth in the sense that parents' life satisfaction will increase compared to baseline levels. This is consistent with Dyrdal and Lucas (2013) who used data from the same GSOEP study. While our results indicated a long-term negative effect in only men, Dyrdal and Lucas (2013) reported negative decreases below baseline in both parents' life satisfaction after the second post-birth year and only when controlling for time-varying changes in respondents' partnership statuses. Differences between the results from their study and our study may be due either to different methodological approaches or due to the different cohorts. While our study included the birth cohorts 2003 to 2009, their study included also older generations of parents (birth cohorts starting with 1986).

Limitations and outlook

There are some limitations of this study. First, we relied on fathers' relative measures of time compared to mothers, but absolute or multidimensional measures (childcare: Pleck, 2010; housework: Minnotte, Stevens, Minnotte, & Kiger, 2007) may play a role as well. For example, fathers' higher engagement in non-routine activities (e.g., play with child; household repairs) may benefit fathers but not mothers.

Second, using GSOEP-data we capture only mothers' ratings, respectively her perception of fathers' support in childcare. The positive association between perceived support and actual involvement may be an indicator of the quality of co-parenting relationships, which implies mutual support between parents in their division of household tasks and child rearing (Feinberg, 2003). Future research is needed to investigate the reliability and validity of support and co-parenting constructs as reported by both parents.

Finally, since we included only cohabitating couples, our findings cannot be generalized to other family constellations. For example, involvement of non-resident fathers with their children may have a different meaning.

Despite these limitations, the present findings contribute to a better understanding of the role of fathers' involvement for couples' transition into parenthood. Our study included longitudinal data and reports from both parents on their time use in housework and childcare and their life satisfaction. Our findings challenge the image we used in the Introduction comparing the trajectories in life satisfaction before and after childbirth with Icarus' flight. In families where fathers were more involved, life-satisfaction trajectories of mothers and fathers were much steeper; both parents had elevated levels around birth and returned to their baseline levels compared to families with less-involved fathers. However, fathers who were less involved did not increase in life satisfaction at birth and decreased below their baseline levels within the third year post-birth. The main practical implication of our study urges a focus on the development of intervention programs centred not only on the event of birth itself, but also on how parents find a joint way of coping with potential difficulties in the years after birth.

REFERENCES

Almeida, D. M., Wethington, E., & McDonald, D. A. (2001). Daily variation in paternal engagement and negative mood: Implications for emotionally supportive and conflictual interactions. *Journal of Marriage and Family, 63*, 417–429. doi:10.1111/j.1741-3737.2001.00417.x.

Asparouhov, T., & Muthén, B. (2010). Bayesian analysis of latent variable models using Mplus. Retrieved from: http://www.statmodel.com/download/BayesAdvantages18.pdf

Bianchi, S., Sayer, L. C., Milkie, M. A., & Robinson, J. P. (2012). Housework: Who did, does or will do it, and how much does it matter? *Social Forces, 91*(1), 55–63. doi:10.1093/sf/sos120.

Cabrera, N. J., Fagan, J., & Farrie, D. (2008). Explaining the long reach of fathers' prenatal involvement on later paternal engagement. *Journal of Marriage and Family, 70*, 1094–1107. doi:10.1111/j.1741-3737.2008.00551.x.

Cabrera, N., Fitzgerald, H. E., Bradley, R. H., & Roggman, L. (2007). Modeling the dynamics of paternal influences on children over the life course. *Applied Development Science, 11*, 185–189. doi:10.1080/10888690701762027.

Clark, A. E., Diener, E., Georgellis, Y., & Lucas, R. E. (2008). Lags and leads in life satisfaction: A test of the baseline hypothesis. *The Economic Journal, 118*, F222–F243. doi:10.1111/j.1468-0297.2008.02150.x.

Cohen, J. (1988). *Statistical power analysis for the behavioral sciences*. Hillsdale, NJ: Lawrence Erlbaum Associates.

Cook, J. L., Jones, R. M., Dick, A. J., & Singh, A. (2005). Revisiting men's role in father involvement: The importance of personal expectations. *Fathering, 3*, 165–178. Retrieved from: http://mensstudies.metapress.com/content/1407285418187275/

Cox, M. J., Paley, B., & Harter, K. (2001). Interparental conflict and parent-child relationships. In J. H. Grych & F. D. Fincham (Eds.), *Interparental conflict and child development: Theory, research, and applications* (pp. 249–272). New York, NY: Cambridge University Press.

Cummings, E. M., Merrilees, C. E., & George, M. W. (2010). Fathers, marriages, and families: Revisiting and updating the framework for fathering in family context. In M. E. Lamb (Ed.), *The role of father in child development* (5th ed., pp. 154–176). Hoboken, NJ: Wiley.

Diener, E., Lucas, R. E., & Scollon, C. N. (2006). Beyond the hedonic treadmill: Revising the adaptation theory of well-being. *American Psychologist, 61*, 305–314. doi:10.1037/0003-066X61.4.305.

Doss, B. D., Rhoades, G. K., Stanley, S. M., & Markman, H. J. (2009). The effect of the transition to parenthood on relationship quality: An 8-year prospective study. *Journal of Personality and Social Psychology, 96*, 601–619. doi:10.1037/a0013969.

Duncan, T. E., Duncan, S. C., & Strycker, L. A. (2006). *Latent variable growth curve modeling.* Mahwah, NJ: Lawrence Erlbaum Associates.

Dyrdal, G. M., & Lucas, R. E. (2013). Reaction and adaptation to the birth of a child: A couple-level analysis. *Developmental Psychology, 49*, 749–761. doi:10.1037/a0028335.

Enders, C. K. (2010). *Applied missing data analysis.* New York, NY: Guilford.

Fagan, J., & Cabrera, N. (2012). Longitudinal and reciprocal associations between coparenting conflict and father engagement. *Journal of Family Psychology, 26*, 1004–1011. doi:10.1037/a0029998.

Feinberg, M. E. (2003). The internal structure and ecological context of parenting: A framework for research and intervention. *Parenting: Science and Practice, 3*, 95–131. doi:10.1207/S15327922PAR0302_01.

Frijters, P., Johnston, D. W., & Shields, M. A. (2011). Life satisfaction dynamics with quarterly life event data. *The Scandinavian Journal of Economics, 113*(1), 190–211. doi:10.1111/j.1467-9442.2010.01638.x.

Goldberg, A. E., & Perry-Jenkins, M. (2004). Division of labor and working-class women's well-being across the transition to parenthood. *Journal of Family Psychology, 18*(1), 225–236. doi:10.1037/0893-3200.18.1.225.

Hansen, T. (2012). Parenthood and happiness: A review of folk theories versus empirical evidence. *Social Indicators Research, 108*, 29–64. doi:10.1007/s11205-011-9865-y.

Holmes, E. K., Cowan, P. A., Cowan, C. P., & Hawkins, A. J. (2012). Marriage, fatherhood and parenting programming. In N. J. Cabrera & C. S. Tamis-LeModa (Eds.), *Handbook of father involvement* (2nd ed., pp. 438–454). New York, NY: Routledge.

Kenny, D. A., Kashy, D. A., & Cook, W. L. (2006). *Dyadic data analysis.* New York, NY: Guilford Press.

Knoester, C., & Eggebeen, D. J. (2006). The effects of the transition to parenthood and subsequent children on men's well-being and social participation. *Journal of Family Issues, 27*, 1532–1560. doi:10.1177/0192513X06290802.

Kühhirt, M. (2012). Childbirth and the long-term division of labour within couples: How do substitution, bargaining power, and norms affect parents' time allocation in West-Germany? *European Sociological Review, 28*, 565–582. doi:10.1093/esr/jcr026.

Lamb, M. E., Pleck, J. H., Charnov, E. L., & Levine, J. A. (1985). Paternal behavior in humans. *American Zoologist, 25*, 883–894.

Lucas, R. E. (2007). Adaptation and the set-point model of subjective well-being: Does happiness change after major life events? *Current Directions in Psychological Science, 16*, 75–79. doi:10.1111/j.1467-8721.2007.00479.x.

Luhmann, M., Hofmann, W., Eid, M., & Lucas, R. E. (2012). Subjective well-being and adaptations to life-events: A meta-analysis on differences between cognitive and affective well-being. *Journal of Personality and Social Psychology, 102*, 592–615. doi:10.1037/a0025948.

Mencarini, L., & Sironi, M. (2012). Happiness, housework and gender inequality in Europe. *European Sociological Review, 28*, 203–219. doi:10.1093/esr/jcq059.

Minnotte, K. L., Stevens, D. P., Minnotte, M. C., & Kiger, G. (2007). Emotion-work performance among dual-earner couples testing four theoretical perspectives. *Journal of Family Issues, 28*, 773–793. doi:10.1177/0192513X07299676.

Muthén, B., & Asparouhov, T. (2012). Bayesian structural equation modeling: A more flexible representation of substantive theory. *Psychological Methods, 17*, 313–335. doi:10.1037/a0026802.

Muthén, L. K., & Muthén, B. O. (1998–2012). *Mplus user's guide. Seventh edition*. Los Angeles, CA: Muthén & Muthén.

Myrskylä, M., & Margolis, R. (2012). Happiness: Before and after the kids. MPIDR Working Paper (WP 2012-013). Retrieved from http://www.demogr.mpg.de/papers/working/wp-2012-013.pdf

Nelson, S. K., Kushlev, K., English, T., Dunn, E. W., & Lyubomirsky, S. (2013). In defense of parenthood: Children are associated with more joy than misery. *Psychological Science, 24*(1), 3–10. doi:10.1177/0956797612447798.

Nomaguchi, K. M., Brown, S. L., & Leyman, T. M. (2012). Father involvement and mothers' parenting stress: The role of relationship status. Fragile Families Working Paper (12-07-FF). Retrieved from: http://www.bgsu.edu/organizations/cfdr/page84100.html

Nomaguchi, K. M., & Milkie, M. A. (2003). Costs and rewards of children: The effects of becoming a parent on adults' lives. *Journal of Marriage and Family, 65*, 356–374. doi: 10.1111/j.1741-3737.2003.00356.x.

Nomaguchi, K. M., Milkie, M. A., & Bianchi, S. M. (2005). Time strains and psychological well-being: Do dual-earner mothers and fathers differ? *Journal of Family Issues, 26*, 756–792. doi: 10.1177/0192513X05277524.

Palkovitz, R., Fagan, J., & Hull, J. (2012). Coparenting and children's well-being. In N. J. Cabrera & C. S. Tamis-LeModa (Eds.), *Handbook of father involvement* (2nd ed., pp. 202–220). New York, NY: Routledge.

Pleck, J. (2010). Paternal involvement: Revised conceptualization and theoretical linkages with child outcomes. In M. E. Lamb (Ed.), *The role of the father in child development* (5th ed., pp. 58–93). Hoboken, NJ: Wiley.

Redshaw, M., & Henderson, J. (2013). Fathers' engagement in pregnancy and childbirth: Evidence from a national survey. *BMC Pregnancy and Childbirth, 13*, 70. doi:10.1186/1471-2393-13-70.

Riina, E. M., & Feinberg, M. E. (2012). Involvement in childrearing and mothers' and fathers' adjustment. *Family Relations, 61*, 836–850. doi:10.1111/j.1741-3729.2012.00739.x.

Schober, P. S. (2012). Paternal child care and relationship quality: A longitudinal analysis of reciprocal associations. *Journal of Marriage and Family, 74*, 281–296. doi:10.1111/j.1741-3737.2011.00955.x.

Vanassche, S., Swicegood, G., & Matthijs, K. (2013). Marriage and children as a key to happiness? Cross-national differences in the effects of marital status and children on well-being. *Journal of Happiness Studies, 14*, 501–524. doi:10.1007/s10902-012-9340-8.

Wagner, G. G., Frick, J. R., & Schupp, J. (2007). The German Socio-Economic Panel study (SOEP): Scope, evolution and enhancements. *Schmollers Jahrbuch, 127*(1), 139–169. Retrieved from: http://www.diw.de/sixcms/detail.php?id=diw_02.c.233221.de

Wical, K. A., & Doherty, W. J. (2005). How reliable are fathers' reports of involvement with their children?: A methodological report. *Fathering: A Journal of Theory, Research, and Practice about Men as Fathers, 3*(1), 81–91. doi:10.3149/fth.0301.81.

Wickham, H. (2009). *ggplot2: Elegant graphics for data analysis*. New York, NY: Springer.

Index

Note: Page numbers followed by 'f' refer to figures and followed by 't' refer to tables.